BASIC ILLUSTRATED
Canoeing

Cliff Jacobson

Illustrations by Lon Levin

FALCONGUIDES®

GUILFORD, CONNECTICUT
HELENA, MONTANA
AN IMPRINT OF THE GLOBE PEQUOT PRESS

To the late Harry Roberts, former editor of *Wilderness Camping and Canoesport Journal*. Harry promoted the joy of fast, lean canoes and was among the first to publicly say that it was okay to "switch sides" when paddling. Harry coined terms like "barking dog," "meat platter," and "dishpan" for slow, inefficient canoes he didn't like. Unimaginative canoe makers took issue but ultimately brought forth better designs!
Harry, we miss your honest love of canoes, your quick wit, and your sharp-tongued downeast humor.

FALCONGUIDES®

Copyright © 2008 by Cliff Jacobson

Text and page design by Karen Williams [intudesign.net]
Photos by Cliff Jacobson unless otherwise noted.

Library of Congress Cataloging-in-Publication Data is available.

ISBN 978-0-7627-4759-7

Printed in the United States of America
First Edition/First Printing

To buy books in quantity for corporate use
or incentives, call **(800) 962–0973,**
or e-mail **premiums@GlobePequot.com.**

Contents

Introduction

Canoeing has changed considerably since the days of wood-ribbed craft and ash beaver-tail paddles. Today's best canoes are faster, sleeker, lighter, and stronger than anything the Native Americans ever built! Family-sized tandem canoes that weigh less than forty-five pounds—and solo canoes that weigh less than thirty pounds!—are a reality. Paddles, too, are lighter, better-balanced, and more energy efficient. Indeed, if you haven't tried a modern wood or ultralight carbon-fiber bent-shaft paddle, you're in for a treat.

Asymmetric hull shapes, which a decade ago were considered chic, are now a feature of nearly all the best canoes. And wood-canvas canoes, which were once a dying breed, are enjoying a strong comeback.

Despite continuing innovation, the basics of how to paddle, pack, and portage canoes have not changed. Canoeists must still be able to paddle a straight course, turn sharply, brace in currents, and execute a host of other maneuvers. And every paddler must know how to avoid rocks, waterfalls, dams, and other dangers.

Why paddle a canoe when kayaks are more popular? Kayaks are like sports cars; canoes range from hot sedans to pick-up trucks. Kayaks emphasize targeted performance at the expense of practicality; canoes are much more versatile. For example, the same canoe that you use for floating gentle rivers can safely carry your family and a week's load of camping gear deep into the wilderness, run twisty creeks and rapids, provide a stable platform for fishing and photographing, and portage easily from pond to pond. You would need several specialized kayaks to do all this!

I won't pretend that this book is a complete treatise on canoeing. No single text this size could be. But everything you need to know to get started right is contained in these pages—and it's all updated to reflect the latest in canoeing equipment, safety procedures and paddling methods.

Bon voyage . . . and may the wind be at your back.

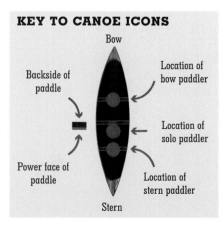

KEY TO CANOE ICONS

Bow

Backside of paddle

Power face of paddle

Location of bow paddler

Location of solo paddler

Location of stern paddler

Stern

Acknowledgments

Thanks to Ted Bell, Mike Cichanowski, Dan Cooke, Craig Johnson, Dave Kruger, Jim Mandle, Bill Ostrom, Bear Paulson, Larry Rice, Tony Way, Brian and Sonja Wieber, and Charlie Wilson. Huge accolades also go out to Bell Canoe Works and We-no-nah Canoe for their technical advice on modern canoe design and construction.

Appreciation goes to these companies for use of selected photos: Chota Outdoor Gear, Bell Canoe Works, Dagger Canoe Company, We-no-nah Canoe Company, Larry Ricker/LHR Images

CHAPTER 1

How to Choose a Canoe

A variety of canoes.

A Primer on Modern Canoe Design

Contrary to popular belief (and the claims of some manufacturers), there's no such thing as a "perfect" canoe—or even an "all-around" canoe. No single watercraft, regardless of its design, materials, or quality of construction, can do everything well.

It's unrealistic to expect a single canoe to win flatwater races on Saturday, clean house in a whitewater slalom on Sunday, and confidently truck the family and 150 pounds of camping gear on a three-week stint across wilderness waters. It's equally absurd to expect this same canoe to weigh forty pounds and hang together when it's wrapped around a midstream boulder. Even if such a canoe existed, its high price would put it out of reach of even the most discriminating paddler. Canoes, like cars, have distinct personalities—a major reason why serious canoeists often own several canoes.

Since I can't put you into the "perfect" canoe—or even the best one for your needs—I'll instead offer some guidelines to help you make some intelligent buying decisions. In the process, I'll suggest some ways to keep you from getting ripped off when you plunk down your hard-earned dollars on a new or used boat. First, here are some terms and design principles to build on. (Note that a complete glossary of canoe terms is found in appendix 1).

Length

Other things being equal, the longer the canoe, the faster it will be. Canoes are *displacement* hulls: Their maximum speed (displacement speed)—which says nothing about the effort required to reach that speed—is determined by the formula S (speed) equals 1.55 times the square root of the waterline length. Simple math reveals that an 18½-foot canoe can be driven 6.7 miles per hour, while a 15-footer can be driven 6.0 miles per hour. A small difference perhaps, but one that can translate into "ease of paddling." Be aware that speed and ease of paddling are not the same. The formula tells you only the *maximum* hull speed, not how much muscle is required to get it there. A sophisticated 16-footer will probably paddle more easily than a workhorse 18-footer. But it will have a lower top speed.

The displacement formula breaks down some in water that is less than 3 feet deep. That's because a hard-pushed canoe produces a substantial bow wave, which is difficult to climb over. The result is loss of speed. Racers refer to this phenomenon as "climbing" and combat its effects by paddling canoes with wide, buoyant sterns. Hence, the development of the asymmetrical canoe—a grand performer in shallows, yet equally formidable in the deep.

RULE ONE: *Other things being equal, the longer the canoe, the faster it will be. And if you want the best shallow-water performance, opt for asymmetry below the waterline.*

Stability and Bottom Shape

Canoes usually have either high *initial* stability (the boat feels steady when it sets flat on the water) and low *final* stability (resistance to capsizing), or vice versa. It's impossible to maximize both variables unless the craft has a very wide molded beam.

High initial stability is best typified by a hull that is very flat in cross-section (see figure 1-2). High final stability is characteristic of a more rounded hull.

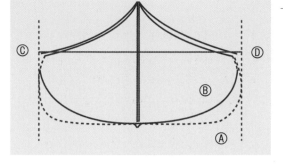

FIGURE 1-1:

The inward curve of the sides of the canoe above the waterline is called tumblehome (canoe A). Canoe B has flared sides, which are much more seaworthy. Note that the maximum beam (C–D) is the same for both canoes.

A flat-bottom canoe at first feels stable, but when heeled past the bilge, turns turtle without warning. On the other hand, round-, vee-, and shallow-arch-bottom canoes (see figure 1-2) feel shaky initially, but they firm up when heeled and thus resist capsizing. In short, rounded hulls are more predictable and controllable than flat ones on all types of water. And they're more easily propelled too!

RULE TWO: *Stability (initial and final), ease of paddling, and seaworthiness are functions of hull shape. The round-, vee-, and shallow-arch-bottom hulls excel in every category except initial stability. A canoe should have high final stability plus enough initial stability so that you can paddle it without fear of capsizing. Unfortunately, most manufacturers boast the "initial stability" of their canoes, the less important of the two variables.*

Keels

An external keel will make any canoe track (hold its course) better. However, it will also act as a cow-catcher in rapids; it'll hang up on rocks and cause upsets.

Let's not mince words. External keels are generally the sign of an inferior canoe design. A canoe that requires an afterthought tacked on below to make it paddle straight belongs back on the redrawing board. Good tracking may be achieved simply by combining a round, shallow-

FIGURE 1-2:

Flat-bottom canoes have high initial stability and low final stability. Round-, vee-, and shallow-arch-bottom canoes usually have the opposite.

Flat Bottom: High initial stability on calm water. Low final stability (may capsize!) in waves and when leaned.

Shallow-arch Bottom: Best all-round hull shape. Very predictable in waves and rapids and when heeled (leaned) to one side. Good initial and final stability.

Shallow Vee Bottom: Similar performance to Shallow Arch but is less efficient due to greater wetted surface. Rides lower in water than Shallow Arch—bottom may catch on rocks.

Round Bottom: Fastest design but very low initial stability (tricky to balance). A feature of some calm water racing canoes.

arch, or vee bottom, narrow ends, a straight keel line (more on this later), and somewhat squarish stems (ends) (see figure 1-5). Aluminum canoes are formed in two halves, so they need a keel to hold the halves together. But even here, the keel could be mounted on the inside of the hull rather than on the outside.

The real reason for keels is to stiffen a floppy bottom. The biggest, flattest canoe bottom can be strengthened considerably by hanging a piece of angle aluminum or one-by-two along its length. Throw in a bunch of ribs and maybe a vertical strut or three—the most shapeless hull will become rigid.

RULE THREE: *Avoid canoes with keels. Exception—aluminum canoes, which don't come any other way. Some aluminum canoe makers offer shallow-draft "shoe" keels on their heavyweight whitewater models. Shoe keels make a lot more sense than the standard T-grip rock grabbers (see figures 1-4 and 1-6).*

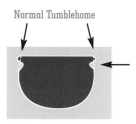

Normal Tumblehome

Shouldered Tumblehome

Cross-section

FIGURE 1-3:

Shouldered Tumblehome.

FIGURE 1-4:

A standard or T-keel.

1. Square stem

2. Slightly rounded stem

FIGURE 1-5.

Canoe 1 has square stems; canoe 2 has rounded stems. Square stems promote straight-line tracking; rounded stems encourage turns.

FIGURE 1-6:

*Canoes with shoe (whitewater)
keels are more maneuverable
and are less likely to catch on
subsurface rocks than similar
models with standard keels.*

Tumblehome

The inward curve of the sides of some canoes is called tumblehome
(see figure 1-1). It's used for two reasons: 1) The curve strengthens the
hull. The alternative to tumblehome may be more ribs, hence more
weight. 2) Tumblehome reduces the width of the canoe at the gunnels
and makes it easier to paddle because you don't have to reach so far
over the sides.

Tumblehome is used in varying degrees on nearly all canoes. But
when you wrap a tight bilge curve, you sacrifice seaworthiness. A fully
flared hull, like that on a wild river dory, is the most seaworthy configu-
ration. But, flaring a canoe from the bottom to the rails would make it
impossibly wide, and therefore uncomfortable to paddle, so all but the
narrowest canoes need some tumblehome. The best canoes have tumblehome at the center and flared bows to deflect waves.

Shouldered tumblehome (also called "shouldered flare"): Here's a
slick variation on tumblehome. If you extend the canoe sides upward to
a double-radiused shoulder, the canoe can be made narrow at the
rails yet flared below (figure 1-3). The advantages of a radiused hull
include:

- Improved seaworthiness: stability *increases* as the hull leans.

- The shouldered curve functions like an I-beam and strengthens the
  sidewall below the rails. Lighter gunnel stock can be used.

- The rails (gunnels) can be mounted perpendicular to the keel line
  and flush with thwarts and seats. This produces a stronger joint
  and a more pleasing look.

A shouldered tumblehome has several real advantages. The canoe is a Bell Wildfire (solo canoe). Note the brightly colored lines coiled on deck.

RULE FOUR: *Seaworthiness suffers if tumblehome extends too far forward or aft. The bow of a tumblehomed canoe should be flared to deflect waves. Shouldered tumblehome is a very good thing!*

Depth

Other things being equal, the deeper the canoe, the drier it will run in rough water. A center depth of around 12-½ inches is plenty for a pleasure canoe, while an inch or two more is standard in wilderness trippers and whitewater craft.

Very shallow depth (less than 12 inches) is permissible in lightly loaded canoes that have seaworthy hull configurations (round, vee, or shallow-arch bottoms with flared sides). Avoid high ends; they merely add weight and act as wind sails.

Beam

Beam is the distance across a boat at its widest point. As you can see in Figure 1-1, "maximum beam" (C–D) may occur at the gunnels (gunnel beam) or someplace lower in the boat (waterline beam). Manufacturers' advertised maximum beam dimensions for canoes A and B would be identical, but the two boats would perform quite differently.

In an effort to provide more meaningful information about the paddling characteristics of their canoes, some manufacturers supply width figures at the 3-inch or 4-inch working waterlines. A narrow waterline usually means a fast, easy-paddling canoe. A wide waterline suggests the opposite.

Professional racing canoes are built to a formula that generally translates to a minimum beam of 27 inches at the 3-inch waterline; United States Canoe Association (USCA) competition cruisers follow the "4-and-32" rule—a 32-inch minimum beam at the 4-inch waterline.

It's probably okay for a wilderness tripping canoe to be wider at the 4-inch waterline than a USCA cruiser. An extra inch or two here might improve load capacity without noticeably affecting performance. On the other hand, it's doubtful you'd want a much beamier hull than a 4-and-32 for general cruising.

RULE FIVE: *If you want to race, buy a canoe built to the appropriate race specifications. Otherwise, begin your search for the ideal hull with canoes where the midsection measures within an inch or so of the 4-and-32 rule. Most canoe manufacturers print 4-inch waterline statistics in their catalogs.*

FIGURE 1-7:

Rocker: The fore and aft upward curve of the keel line of a canoe is called rocker. Rockered canoes turn more easily than those without rocker.

Whitewater canoes need lots of rocker for maneuverabilitly in rapids. Canoe is a Dagger Ocoee.

Rocker

The fore and aft upward curve of the keel line of a canoe is called rocker. A highly rockered canoe will turn more easily and rise more quickly to oncoming waves than a similar canoe without rocker. But it won't track as well, which means you'll need to correct its course more frequently.

Racers like a canoe with near zero rocker. Whitewater canoes should have severe rocker—4 or more inches is not uncommon. A touring canoe or wilderness tripper might fall somewhere in between—about 1 to 3 inches. The important thing to consider is how the boat will be used. A canoe that tracks straight when empty will turn reluctantly when heavily loaded. A heavy load forces a canoe down into the water (acting like a keel) and so improves tracking. Wilderness canoes ordinarily are heavily loaded and therefore require some rocker. Conversely, it makes little sense to have more than about 3 inches of rocker in a minimally loaded day cruiser.

The amount of rocker a canoe needs depends largely on its length and hull shape. Generally, short canoes need less rocker than long ones, and flat-bottomed canoes need less rocker than shallow-arch and vee-bottomed ones. Straight-keeled canoes can be turned easily by simply leaning them on their sides (you use the rocker in the sidewall).

Asymetrical (progressive) rocker: Most canoes have "symmetrical"

High volume Bell Alaskan Royalex canoe loaded for a two week trip on the upper Missouri River. Note full spray cover which deters rain and waves. (Photo: Dennis Davidson)

FIGURE 1-8:

Capacity figures alone tell you nothing about how a canoe will perform when heavily loaded. Here, canoe 1 will handle a load much better than canoe 2 because its wide buoyant ends will rise over waves rather than knife dangerously through them. But canoe 2 is the faster of the two canoe types, all other things equal. Flaring the bows of canoe 2—so they'll turn away waves—will significantly increase seaworthiness.

rocker—the rise is the same at both ends. But the trend is toward "progressive" rocker—there's more lift at the bow than at the stern. Consider these benefits: When a canoe is paddled forward, its bow meets more resistance than the stern (which is essentially in calm water). You can reduce this resistance by adding more lift (rocker) to the bow. But, if you add a similar amount of rocker to the stern to compensate, you amplify the craft's tendency to wander off course (a deeply planted stern acts like a directional skeg, or short vertical fin).

What to do? The solution is to increase bow rocker and decrease stern rocker. This will improve tracking without appreciably affecting maneuverability.

RULE SIX: *Figure on near zero rocker for a racer, 1 or 2 inches for a day cruiser, and up to 3 inches for a wilderness tripper. For whitewater boats, the more rocker the merrier. Remember, how the rocker is applied—whether uniform or symmetrical—makes a difference.*

Trim

Canoes are designed to perform best when they are trimmed dead level—that is, the bow and stern ride equally high in the water. If the bow is trimmed down, the stern will tend to scoot sideways when you paddle—you'll constantly correct the course. If the stern is trimmed down, the tail will dig in like a skeg and make the canoe hard to turn. The point is that your canoe must be trimmed dead level to take proper advantage of its built-in rocker!

Capacity

The advertised carrying capacity of a canoe is generally meaningless information. That's because about three-fourths of a canoe's load-carrying ability is borne by the middle third of its length (figure 1-8). Moreover, capacity figures tell you nothing about seaworthiness or how the canoe will perform when heavily loaded. In the example below, canoe 1 is much more seaworthy than canoe 2 because its wide

The author repairs the split ends of a Royalex Canoe along the North Knife River, Manitoba, near Hudson Bay.

buoyant ends will rise over waves rather than knife through them. But canoe 2 is definitely the faster of the two.

RULE SEVEN: *Advertised load capacities are generally meaningless. If you want a load carrier, select a hull with a profile similar to canoe 1. If you want speed, choose a canoe with finer ends. Note that it's impossible to improve on both variables—speed and capacity—without changing the length of the canoe. That's why long canoes carry loads more effortlessly than short ones.*

Weight and Strength

You can have a strong canoe or a light canoe, but it's unlikely you can have both unless you choose a very sophisticated and frightfully expensive ($2,000 plus) lay-up.

Leading-edge manufacturers are using aircraft technology to make canoes lighter, stiffer, and stronger. For example, the 18-foot family-sized We-no-nah Champlain weighs just forty-five pounds in ultralight Kevlar construction. Solo canoes are lighter still: my favorite—a Kevlar Bell Yellowstone solo—weighs just twenty-nine pounds! Royalex canoes too, have shaved pounds.

Advertised weights of aluminum, Kevlar, and fiberglass composite canoes are pretty accurate. Royalex canoes show more variation because the plastic sheets used in the construction vary slightly in weight. Gunnel stock makes a difference: aluminum is usually the lightest, followed by vinyl, then wood. Color counts on Kevlar composite boats—some pigments weigh more than others. Exceptions abound. Take your bathroom scale with you when you go canoe shopping.

RULE EIGHT: *You can have an ultralight and strong canoe only if you choose a very sophisticated and expensive lay-up.*

Abrasion

Canoes generally die of abrasion, not from being wrapped around rocks. The harder the canoe's material, the better it will resist abrasion. Heat-treated aluminum ranks number one in the "drag it through the shallows" category, with polyethylene, ABS plastic, and Kevlar

No canoe is indestructible! The author found this abandoned aluminum canoe below a falls on Ontario's Kopka River.

composite boats not far behind. Next comes Royalex, followed by wood-strip and wood-canvas canoes.

Ease of Repair

If you use a canoe hard, you'll ultimately need to repair it. Canoes built of fiberglass and Kevlar are easiest to repair; a properly applied patch is hardly noticeable. Wood-strip canoes mend nicely, as do ABS Royalex and wood-canvas ones. Aluminum canoes can be repaired, but the patch will be a glaring reminder of the rock you hit. Patching polyethylene canoes is beyond the ability of most novices.

A well-kept Kevlar composite canoe may increase in value! Canoe is a We-no-nah Prism. (Photo: Chota Outdoor Gear)

Despite what some canoe manufacturers say, no canoe-building material is indestructible. So consider the merits of a less durable canoe that is easily patched over a more durable one that is not.

> **RULE NINE:** *No canoe is indestructible! Generally, the more durable the canoe material, the more difficult it will be to effect an invisible repair, and vice versa.*

Longevity

How long a new canoe lasts depends on how much you use (and abuse) it, the amount of exposure to ultraviolet light, and the material from which it is built. Some materials have a longer lifespan than others. Here are some industry averages: polyethylene lasts about eight years; Royalex, thirteen years; composites, twenty-seven years;

On Buying a Used Canoe

1. Know the current retail price of the canoe before you buy it. Good canoes command around 80 percent of their current market value; cheapies 10 to 20 percent less.

2. Stay away from the classified ads in newspapers, unless you want a typical aluminum or polyethylene canoe. High-tech canoes are almost never advertised in newspapers. If brand names are not specified in the ad, you can bet the canoe is junk.

3. Canoe races and paddling seminars are good places to frequent if you want a good buy on a used canoe. Canoe enthusiasts want their old "friends" to go to other enthusiasts, not to "canoers" who would rather fish than paddle.

4. Home-built canoes may be good or bad. The good ones are built on club forms and are advertised almost exclusively in canoe club newsletters and by word of mouth. The bad ones are usually constructed from plans supplied in popular magazines and are invariably advertised in newspapers.

5. Turn used canoes upside down and sight along the keel line. Don't buy a canoe with a "hogged" (bent-in) keel line. Once a keel line is bent, it's almost impossible to straighten properly.

6. Check fiberglass/Kevlar canoes for signs of hull delamination. A cloudy matrix tells the tale. Once delamination begins, it usually continues. Avoid these boats like the plague!

7. Don't overreact to minor surface damage: Galled varnish, scratched gel-coat, and surface cracks in woodwork are easily repairable. But don't buy a canoe with a twisted stem, broken gunnel, or hull that's out-of-round.

8. If a canoe looks out-of-round or twisted when you stand back a ways and view it, it probably is. Your eyes are a most accurate measuring device!

9. Good canoes *appreciate*. Bad ones do the opposite. You can't go wrong by buying a good used canoe.

wood-and-canvas canoes never die—they just accumulate new parts; aluminum canoes may live forever.

Value Per Dollar

Bad canoes *depreciate*. Good ones *appreciate*! A polyethylene or ABS plastic canoe in good condition may lose 70 percent of its original value after just five years; a Royalex or aluminum canoe, perhaps half. A well-kept Kevlar composite or wood-canvas canoe may *increase* in value. Home-built canoes and fiberglass-covered wood-strip canoes (even those in mint condition) depreciate rapidly—they can be a good deal if you want one.

Solo Canoe Considerations

The traditional requirements for length, depth, and beam mentioned earlier don't apply to solo canoes. Most variables (speed, tracking, turning, portability, seaworthiness, and general handiness) will be maximized in a canoe length of 14 to16 feet, an outwale (outside edge of the gunnel) beam of 27 to 30 inches, and a center depth of 11 to 12 inches. Except for use in severe whitewater, additional depth is unnecessary, since the paddler is located at the craft's fulcrum. It takes a very big rapid to bury the ends of even a low-volume solo canoe.

CHAPTER 2

How They're Built

A Lesson in Fabrics, Resins, and Materials

Used to be you could choose from wood-canvas, aluminum, and fiberglass canoes. Add lapstrake, plywood, and wood-strip boats, and you defined the product line. Now, there are a wealth of exotic new materials and equally exotic ways of using them.

Royalex

Around 1960, UniRoyal began to offer foam-cored ABS plastic to the canoe industry. And the Royalex canoe was born. It's been growing strong ever since. Royalex is a thermoplastic

Kevlar canoes are lightweight, strong, and beautiful. The author paddles his Bell Wildfire solo canoe. (Photo: Sue Harings)

Royalex canoes slide over rocks with barely a rumor! Note that the lining ropes are secured low on the stem of the canoe. The short spray cover cuts wind and keeps out splash.

laminate with an approximately half-inch-thick blown plastic core. The number and thickness of laminations is specified by the canoe maker. Some Royalex lay-ups are quite substantial, others are merely adequate. You get what you pay for! An outer sheath of colored cross-linked vinyl protects the ABS from decomposing in the sun.

Royalex is extremely tough and slippery: It will slide over rocks that would stop aluminum canoes in their tracks and break or damage fiberglass or Kevlar craft. And Royalex has an excellent "memory": Wrap your canoe around a bridge piling and it'll probably pop back into shape with scarcely a crease.

Royalex can withstand severe impact but only limited abrasion. Continued dragging through shallows will reduce the smooth vinyl skin to a mass of deep cuts. Nonetheless, the product is incredibly durable—the favorite of whitewater daredevils.

Early Royalex canoes had fairly inefficient shapes because manufacturers couldn't mold the thick Royalex sheet into tight curves. But that problem has largely been solved—today's best Royalex canoes now mimic the slick look of their composite cousins. Yes, composites still have the edge, but Royalex makers are closing in.

Kevlar

In the early 1970s, DuPont developed a honey-gold tire-cord fabric (now used widely in policemen's flak vests) they called Kevlar. Some world-class whitewater paddlers built canoes and kayaks from the material and were so impressed by its strength they nicknamed it "holy cloth." Today Kevlar is the staple fabric in every high-performance canoe and kayak and is also widely used to reinforce selected areas of stock fiberglass canoes.

Kevlar is about 40 percent stronger than fiberglass and not quite half as light. It's very difficult to puncture or tear. Unlike fiberglass, Kevlar cannot be sanded; it just frizzes up like cotton candy. Run a Kevlar hull persistently over sharp rocks and the bottom will look like it needs a haircut. Repairing the mess requires painting on resin (epoxy, vinylester, or polyester) and cutting off and wet-sanding the resin while it is "green." The alternative is to cover the damaged area with a fiber-glass patch which, when dry, can be sanded smooth.

The trend today is away from single-laminate (all-Kevlar construc-tion). Top-of-the-line canoe makers now blend canoe materials like steel alloys, taking advantage of today's knowledge of what works best, where. There are dozens, perhaps hundreds, of proprietary lay-ups that use fiberglass, Kevlar, nylon, Dacron, carbon fiber, closed-cell foams, and other materials in a dazzling array of configurations.

A family-sized Kevlar canoe. Foam-rib Kevlar composite canoes are ideal for lake country canoe routes that have long portages. They are not strong enough for serious rapids.

Gel-coat is an abrasion-resistant waterproof resin that's used on the outside of most Kevlar canoes. The black canoe in front has a clear gel-coat; the one behind it has a red gel-coat. Gel-coats (regardless of color) "scratch white" when the canoe hits rocks. The author prepares to portage out of a mucky pond along the Steel River, Ontario. Note spray covers and coiled lines on deck. (Photo: Gary McGuffin)

Clear (natural gold-colored) Kevlar degrades in sunlight. A colored gel coat protects best, or you can apply a chemical, like 303 Protectant, that is an ultraviolet barrier.

Fiberglass

Fiberglass is not as durable as aluminum, Royalex, polyethylene, or Kevlar, but it's plenty strong enough for a recreational canoe, even one that will be used in rapids. Fiberglass canoes can be good or bad, depending on how they are built. These terms will help you understand the differences.

Fiberglass cloth: Composed of twisted strands of fiberglass woven at right angles to one another, fiberglass cloth has the highest glass-to-resin ratio (about 1:1) of all the fiberglass materials, and also the greatest strength. The best fiberglass canoes are built of all-cloth laminates.

Matt: Chopped cross-linked glass fibers held together with a dried resin binder. Matt has a glass-to-resin ratio of about 1:3, which means it's a third as strong as cloth. Matt absorbs a lot of resin and adds stiffness to a hull, so it's regularly used in canoe bilges where extreme rigidity is desirable. Matt is cheaper than cloth, and it's much heavier. Most good canoes are stiffened with additional layers of cloth (more expensive) or roving rather than matt.

Roving: Similar to cloth but with a coarser weave. Glass-to-resin ratio is slightly less than cloth, but impact resistance is greater. Many of the best canoes utilize some roving as a stiffener.

E-glass and S-glass: E-glass is a common boat-building fabric that can be purchased at any marina. S-glass—a patterned material—is much more abrasion-resistant and expensive. Some (mostly home built) whitewater canoes have a layer of S-glass on the outside to better resist scrapes.

Gel-coat: This is an abrasion-resistant waterproof resin that is used on the outside of most fiberglass and Kevlar canoes. To save weight, some high-performance canoes are built without gel-coat; this is called skin-coat (or "resin-coat") construction. Skin-coat boats are less resistant to abrasion and ultraviolet light than those with gel-coat.

Canoe-Building Resins

Polyester: Inexpensive, not very strong, and a standard of the canoe-building industry.

Vinylester: Stronger, more flexible, and only slightly more expensive than polyester. Many of the best Kevlar canoes are built with Vinylester resins.

Epoxy: The strongest and most expensive of all resins. It is difficult to work with, and it's more toxic than polyester or vinylester. Epoxy boats are harder to patch than vinylester boats, and they degrade more in sunlight. Whether epoxy has enough advantages over vinylester to warrant its higher cost is debatable.

Construction Lay-ups

Chopper-gun lay-up: A mixture of chopped strands of fiberglass and polyester resin is sprayed into a mold. The resulting canoe is very heavy, not very strong, and cheap. All the worst canoes are built this way. The telltale matrix of chopped fibers is visible on the inner walls of the craft. Chopper-gun canoes have largely disappeared from the North American market. They are no bargain at any price!

Hand lay-ups: Fiberglass cloth, and perhaps roving and matt, are laid into the mold by hand and saturated with resin, then squeezed dry. You can see the cloth gridwork on the inside walls of the boat. A lot of very good fiberglass and Kevlar canoes are built this way.

Vacuum bagging: A plastic "vacuum bag" is placed into the mold and the air is pumped out. A vacuum cleaner was originally used as the power source—hence the name. The bag compresses the resin-soaked laminate and evenly distributes every ounce of resin so there are no pooled spots that add weight. This method produces the highest cloth-to-resin ratio possible. The very best canoes are built this way.

Foam Cores

A canoe bottom that flexes due to water pressure won't maintain its shape and paddling efficiency. For this reason, performance-minded canoeists prefer hulls that are as stiff as possible. The lightest, strongest way to stiffen a canoe is to sandwich a layer of closed-cell foam between the Kevlar laminates. Often, foam ribs are added to increase the tortional stiffness of the sidewalls. The entire boat is then vacuum-bagged to eliminate as much resin (and weight) as possible.

But there are concerns: a recreational canoe needs some flex so its bottom won't break when it hits rocks. Early foam-cored canoes often broke or delaminated on impact. But modern cored canoes are much more rugged. If you're willing to sacrifice some strength in return for ultimate lightness and superior stiffness, a foam-core canoe may be right for you. Over the years, I've owned three foam-core solo canoes, all of which have been used on tough Ontario rivers. Scratches and patches? Yes. Delamination? Never!

Let's summarize what we've learned about fiberglass and Kevlar construction:

1. All-Kevlar canoes aren't as durable as those constructed from hybrid laminates. And they're much more expensive.
2. Foam cores are ideal where light weight is the primary consideration. They are not strong enough for serious rapids.
3. Vinylester resin offers the best compromise between low cost and high strength/durability.
4. A recreational canoe should have a gel-coat for abrasion protection. Skin-coat canoes won't take much abuse.
5. The cheapest canoes are built with chopper guns. The best are hand-laid or vacuum-bagged.

Aluminum

Aluminum canoes aren't dead yet, but the darkness is closing in. Synthetics now rule the market where aluminum was once king. Nonetheless, aluminum remains a good canoe-building material, largely because it is lightweight, inexpensive, and takes abrasion better than plastics or wood. Aluminum canoes are the only canoes that can be left out in the weather all year round.

Aluminum canoes aren't dead yet, but the darkness is closing in. Tip: metal canoes will slide over rocks more easily if you apply a coat of automobile paste to the hull before you go canoeing.

Most aluminum canoe designs are decades old—some date back to the 1940s. Few are very good. The 18-½-foot Alumacraft-canoe (sixty-seven pounds), which was designed with help from the Minnesota Canoe Association, is the best paddling aluminum canoe currently in production.

Aluminum tends to stick to rocks—a characteristic that can be reduced by applying paste wax to the hull. Dents become battle scars that remain forever.

Polyethylene

Polyethylene canoes are strong, reasonably abrasion-resistant, inexpensive, and heavy. Polyethylene works better for decked whitewater canoes and kayaks (the deck stiffens the hull) than for open canoes, which need a foam core (such as Old Town Discovery canoes) or internal bracing (such as Coleman and Pelican canoes) to maintain their shape. Both options add weight.

Polyethylene is very slick and hard to dent; it slides over rocks without

Polyethelene canoes are strong, inexpensive and heavy. Repairing damage is beond the ability of most amateurs.

Many believe that nothing paddles as nicely as a wood-canvas canoe. Certainly, few canoes are as beautiful. Here, the author's friend, Jim Mandle, paddles his restored Henry Rushton built "Indian Girl" canoe—circa 1910.

a sound. Heavy dents, however, may set permanently. Repairing a crack or hole is beyond the ability of most amateurs. The main advantage of polyethylene is its low cost and resistance to damage.

Wood-Canvas Canoes

Wood-canvas canoes are beautiful and practical. Beyond the pride of ownership and the belief that "absolutely nothing paddles like a wood-ribbed canoe," there is resale value—these canoes appreciate considerably over time. Cedar-canvas canoes are easily damaged so they are best kept out of rapids. Still, they are strong enough for an expedition if you paddle well and don't abuse them. Repairing damaged canvas, ribs, and planking is an expected part of owning one of these canoes.

Cedar-Strip Canoes

Many of the canoes that win long-distance flat-water races are hand-built of cedar strips, nailed to a form, glued together, and covered with fiberglass cloth and polyester or epoxy resin (the nails are removed prior to glassing). The resulting canoe is light, beautiful, and much

Cedar strip canoes are beautiful, light and stronger than most people believe. Building plans are available from the Minnesota Canoe Association (www.canoe-kayak.org).

Folding canoes look fragile but they're not. These "go anywhere" canoes fold to fit inside a large duffle bag. They assemble in minutes and paddle much like hard-shelled canoes. (Photo: Scansport Pakboats)

stronger than most people think. As with all wooden boats, these canoes are expensive.

Folding Canoes

These canoes can be assembled in thirty minutes and will fit inside the trunk of a car. They are about 15 percent lighter than hard-shelled canoes. Folding canoes are much tougher than they look—they barely show scratches even after hours of dragging through rocky shallows.

Inflatable canoes are faster and more controllable than rafts, but they are slower and less responsive than hard-shelled canoes. (Photo: Larry Rice)

I've used them on tough Canadian rivers and have yet to apply a patch! Scansport (www.pakboats.com) is the only United States manufacturer of folding canoes.

Inflatable Canoes

Inflatable canoes are much faster and more controllable than rafts, but they are slower and less responsive than hard-shelled canoes—you have to choreograph long-distance moves. But they literally turn on a dime! For big waves and huge holes, they are superior to any hardshell or folding canoe.

CHAPTER 3

Canoe Accessories and Conveniences

If you're new to canoeing, you may not realize just how much gear is required to outfit even a short float trip down a local stream. Besides the obvious—life jackets (also known as PFDs) and paddles for everyone—you'll need cartop carriers, ropes for "tie-downs," a sponge and bailer, "painters" (ropes for mooring the canoe), waterproof gear bags, a first-aid kit, and perhaps specialized items like a carrying yoke and knee pads.

Fortunately, you don't need everything right now. All that's absolutely essential is a canoe, paddle, and life vest, and some way to get it all to the river. Nonetheless, there are a number of low-cost extras which will add measurably to your safety and fun. And these you'll want to get as soon as possible. Here's what you *really* need:

Paddles

Given the choice between propelling a good canoe with a bad paddle or vice versa, I'd have to think on it. You just can't do good work with a shaved-down two-by-four!

Choosing a paddle according to your height has no rational basis because you sit, not stand, in a canoe. Upper-body length and the height of your canoe seat are the major factors in determining paddle length. If you want to be scientific about choosing a paddle:

1. Set your canoe in the water and climb aboard.

2. Measure the distance from your nose (height of the top grip) to the water. That's the shaft length. To this add the length of the blade (20 to 25 inches, depending on paddle style). That's the correct length for you. Note that the overall length of the paddle is in part programmed by the blade length.

If this procedure sounds too much like work, try these paddle lengths for starters: For typical aluminum and Royalex canoes—56 to 60 inches. For high-performance fiberglass/Kevlar cruisers—52 to 55 inches.

Bent paddles: These have blades offset 5 to 15 degrees (12- and 14-degree bends are the most popular). Bent-shafts are much more efficient than straight paddles because their forward angled blades don't "lift" water (and waste power) at the end of the stroke. All effort goes into forward motion.

Bent-shafts are the choice for making time on flat water and for gentle cruising. Don't use 'em for whitewater though; they're too awkward. Your bent-shaft paddle should be about two inches shorter than the straight paddle you favor.

The best paddles are constructed from carefully laminated woods and have tip protectors of polyurethane or Kevlar. The lighter the paddle, the better! Jet-black carbon-fiber racing paddles are the lightest

FIGURE 3-1:

Why the bent paddle is more efficient: Note that the thrust is nearly straight back. A straight paddle "lifts" water at the end of the stroke, which slows the speed of the canoe.

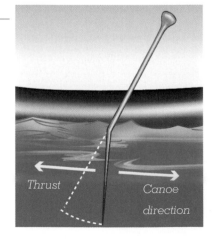

Thrust

Canoe direction

(8 to 14 ounces) paddles of all. You won't find top-grade paddles in hardware stores or marinas. You will find them in specialty canoe and kayak shops and on the Internet. Expect to pay over $100 for a really fine canoe paddle.

How to hold your paddle: Most people grasp too far down on the shaft when they should be choking up. There should be two to three hands of distance (roughly equal to the freeboard of your canoe) between your lower hand and the throat of the paddle. Choking up reduces leverage, but it significantly increases reach—and control.

Life Jackets (PFDs)

It should go without saying that anyone who canoes should wear a life vest. Always! "Canoeists" almost never break this rule. "Canoers" seldom follow it at all. A good PFD is the most important safety edge you can have. Buy a good one!

Try the jacket for fit as follows: Zipper and/or cinch the ties, then grasp the vest by the shoulders and pull it up as high as you can. Does the jacket ride up over your ears? If so, keep shopping; it will perform likewise when you capsize.

A good PFD is the most important safety edge you can have. The author (right) scouts a rapid along the North Knife River in Manitoba.

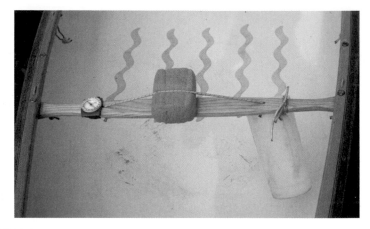

FIGURE 3-2:

Shock-cord strung through holes in thwarts keeps sponge and oddities in place. Note wrist compass attached to thwart.

Life jackets for kids: Proper sizing is even more important here, as youngsters have little body fat (low buoyancy), and their weight is distributed differently than adults. Religiously follow the manufacturer's sizing guidelines and have the youngster try the jacket in a pool. Absolutely never put an adult life vest on a small child. Drowning could result!

Don't compress life jackets when you store them or leave them in hot car trunks; the foam may harden and disintegrate.

Duct Tape

A roll of duct tape should accompany you on every canoe trip. Use it to fix everything from damaged canoes to holed tents. Duct tape is the canoeist's gray badge of courage.

Nylon Ropes and Fabric-Covered Shock-Cord

Most essential is 100 feet of quarter-inch nylon rope. Cut the rope (singe raw ends with a lighter) into 15-foot lengths and coil each piece neatly. Four coils will do permanent duty as "tie-downs" for the canoe;

two will serve admirably as bow and stern painters. Whatever is left will come in handy for something. You can never have too much rope on a canoe trip!

Also, buy about 6 feet of fabric-covered shock-cord. Thread lengths of shock-cord through holes in decks and thwarts (figure 3-2) to provide security for your coiled painters and sundries. Ropes should never be left loose in a canoe where they can wind about your arms and legs in a capsize.

Loose lines and a rough sea don't mix! Shock cords strung through holes in the decks keep coiled lines secure. Note that the lining hole on this canoe is installed half way down the stem. This location provides good control when lining the canoe around obstacles in the river. Do you see the friendly green "alien" on the deck?

Waterproof Gear Bag

For casual float trips, any reasonably watertight container will do. Later, when you get serious about canoeing, you can consider the purchase of sophisticated pack sacks and waterproof bags.

Inexpensive containers that are acceptably waterproof include plastic ice chests and ice-cream buckets (duct-tape the lids shut to make them capsize-proof), heavy-duty—4 to 6 mil—plastic bags, and rubberized laundry bags. Plastic bags should be sandwiched between more durable nylon or canvas bags so they won't be punctured inside or out. An inexpensive burlap or polypropylene sack makes a good abrasion liner for the inside of a pack or duffel.

Security: Drill three sixteenth-inch diameter holes at 6-inch intervals along the inwales (inside gunnels) of your canoe and thread loops of parachute cord through the holes. When rough water threatens, tie in your gear! Use the chute cord loops to anchor your equipment tie-ins.

FIGURE 3-3:

A solo canoe must have a removable yoke—a bolted-in one would interfere with the central paddling position. Note foam knee pads (glued-in), insulated seat pad and sponge secured (with bungee cord) to seat frame.

Yoke

You'll want a yoke even if your canoeing is limited to local waters with no real portages (see figure 3-3). Putting the canoe on and off your car, carrying it to the waterfront etc., often must be done alone. At these times you'll wish you had a genuine yoke! Carrying even a light canoe on a pair of paddles tied between thwarts, as recommended by some "experts," borders on insanity, even for those who relish pain.

The most comfortable setup is a curved wood yoke with oversize (4½ inches by 8 inches) foam-padded shoulder blocks. Make your yoke from white ash and secure it to the gunnels with two bolts at each end. Exception:

A bolted-in yoke on a tandem canoe. Note that yoke is double-bolted to the rails for added security. Single bolted yokes often crack in the vicinity of the bolt.

A solo canoe, like the one pictured in figure 3-3, must have a removable yoke—a bolted-in one would interfere with the central paddling position.

Kneeling Pads

These are necessary only if you're deadly serious about paddling whitewater. The cheapest (and best) pads are 12-inch squares cut from a closed-cell foam (ethyl-vinyl-acetate and neoprene are preferred foams) sleeping pad. Glue knee pads into the hull with contact cement. Foam knee pads are available at canoeing shops.

A factory installed foot brace is common on high performance canoes. (Photo: LHR Images)

Lining Holes

All canoes have some sort of hole or ring at each end for attachment of auto tie-down ropes and tracking lines. Ideally, ropes should be attached as close to the waterline of the canoe as possible to ensure good control when working the craft around obstacles in the river.

The solution is to drill a hole about 4 to 6 inches below the deck plate and epoxy in a length of half-inch-diameter PVC water pipe. The tube will keep water from leaking into the canoe when the bow plunges in rapids and will provide plenty of room for passage of the rope.

Foot Braces

Foot braces lock you firmly into the canoe when you paddle from a sitting position. The simplest brace consists of a pair of wood rails fiberglassed to the floor of the canoe. Alternatively, an aluminum tube, fastened at the ends, is screwed to the rails. (See figure 3-4.) Most slick paddling canoes come with a factory installed footbrace in the stern. Bow paddlers can brace their feet against the bow flotation tank.

Seat Height and Placement

I have yet to own a canoe whose seats were placed where I prefer. Seats on fine-lined cruisers are usually mounted low for stability rather than high for efficiency and all-day comfort.

Many of the best canoes have a sliding bow seat that solves the trim problem when paddlers of different weights are aboard. But few canoes have seats that are adjustable for height. Some paddlers prefer a high mounted seat; others like a low one. Seats that are secured to one-piece drops or individual dowels can be moved; those that are riveted to the sidewalls of the canoe can't!

FIGURE 3-4:

Foot braces lock you firmly into the canoe when you paddle from a sitting position. The simplest brace consists of a pair of wood rails fiberglassed to the floor of the canoe. An aluminum tube, fastened at the ends is screwed to the rails.

CHAPTER 4

Carrying and Cartopping

Your Canoe

Every canoe trip includes some sort of portage—be it the task of loading the canoe onto the car, carrying it to and from the launching site, or lifting it over obstacles in a local stream. And if you're off to the wilds of Canada, portaging is part of the daily routine!

Contrary to popular belief, portaging is more an art than a feat of physical strength. I've seen ninety-pound girls lift seventy-five-pound canoes single-handedly and carry them nonstop a

A properly tied down canoe. Note the heavy duty straps. This paddler takes no changes!

quarter mile over very rough trails. And I've known 180-pound men who could not carry the same canoe more than 100 feet without dropping it on the nearest boulder!

Surprisingly, it's almost always easier to carry a canoe alone than with a friend. That's because partners can rarely coordinate their movements. Two-person carries are only efficient on groomed trails, and then only when the canoe is outfitted with a yoke at each end.

Except in wind, a healthy adult can usually manage a canoe of reasonable weight without help if he or she has a good yoke and knows the correct lift procedures. The improved One-Person Lift illustrated on the next page is by far the easiest method.

Procedure

1. Roll the canoe on its side and grasp the yoke center with your right hand (figure 4-1).
2. Spin the canoe to your thighs by lifting upward on the yoke. As the canoe comes up, your left hand grasps the far gunnel *forward* of the yoke; your right hand moves to near gunnel *behind* it. Nearly all the weight of the canoe is supported by your thighs (figure 4-2).
3. A forceful shove of your right knee and a snap of your arms brings the canoe to your shoulders. Simple as pie . . . *if* you're quick about it! (figures 4-3, 4-4).

Two-person lift: If you want to conserve energy, try the Two-Person Lift. It's identical to the illustrated method except that your helper stands next to you behind the yoke, and you stand slightly in front of it. The canoe should be supported on the thighs of both you and your partner prior to raising it into position. Your hands will be forward of the yoke; and your partner's will be behind it. Raise the canoe on signal together. Easy!

End lift: The end lift—where two partners lift the canoe by rolling it up on one end, should be avoided if you care about the cosmetics of your craft. Every time you roll up, the grounded end of the canoe (apex of the deck plate) takes a beating. Use this method on grass if you like, but avoid it on rocky ground and cement driveways.

FIGURE 4-1:

One-Person Lift. Step 1. Right hand grasps the yoke center and spins the canoe to thighs.

FIGURE 4-2:

Step 2. Left hand grasps top gunwales forward of the yoke and canoe is balanced on thighs. Note location of right hand.

FIGURE 4-3:

Step 3. With a quick upward push from your right knee, snap the canoe up and around over your head.

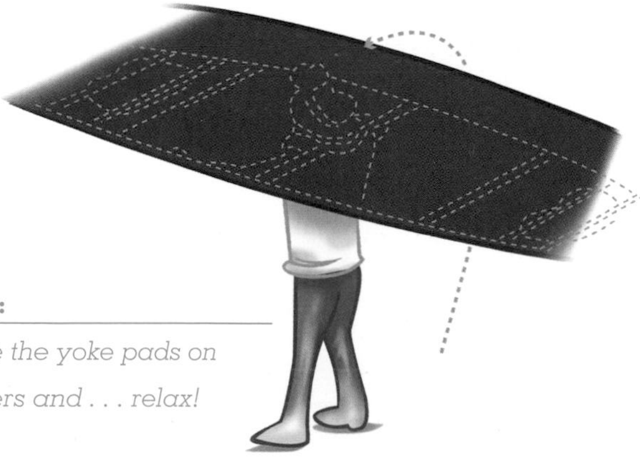

FIGURE 4-4:

Step 4. Settle the yoke pads on your shoulders and . . . relax!

Cartopping Your Canoe

Given enough rope, anyone can tie down a canoe so it won't blow off a car. The fun comes when you've got several boats to haul, or when the wind whips up to impressive speeds. Here are the proven procedures for "event-free" cartopping.

Equipment: If you're fortunate enough to have a car with rain gutters, get canoe racks that bolt directly to them. Avoid suction-cup styles that put pressure on the roof. If your car has airplane-style doors, get racks that are designed *specifically* for them. A generic setup is not good enough! Special brackets are available for gutterless trucks and those with toppers.

Canoe racks *must* be carpeted to prevent galling the canoe's gunnels. Racks that utilize 1-inch tubular steel conduit may be sheathed in heater hose. Just lubricate the metal pipe with brake fluid and the hose will slide right on.

Tie-downs: Straps or ropes? Most experienced canoeists prefer ropes to straps. Why? No one will steal ropes that are left tied to the racks while you're paddling. And, ropes don't have buckles that can damage your car when they're tossed over your cartopped canoe. Cinching ropes takes seconds, if you use the right knots. The "power cinch" (also called the "trucker's knot") is the right hitch for the job. Straps are best for trailered canoes and for those who can't tie knots.

FIGURE 4-5:

For cars that don't have rain gutters— secure your tie-downs to loops of nylon webbing attached to a bracket or bolt under the hood of your car.

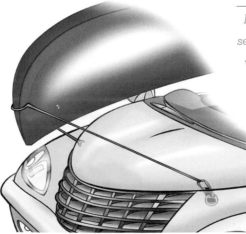

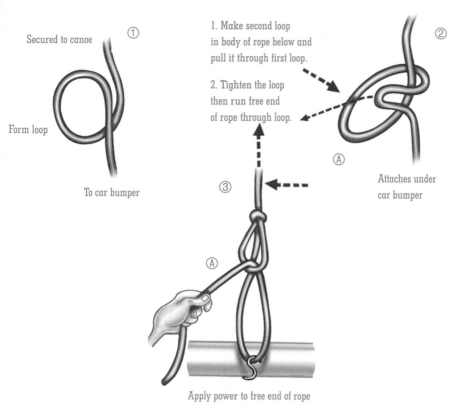

Secured to canoe

① Form loop

To car bumper

1. Make second loop in body of rope below and pull it through first loop.

2. Tighten the loop then run free end of rope through loop.

②

Ⓐ

Attaches under car bumper

③

Ⓐ

Apply power to free end of rope

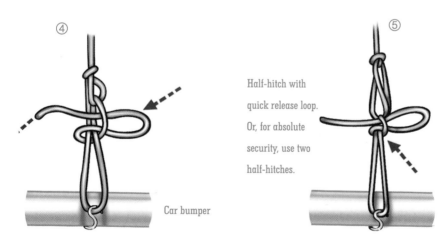

④

Car bumper

Half-hitch with quick release loop. Or, for absolute security, use two half-hitches.

⑤

FIGURE 4-6:

Power Cinch Sequence.

Rules for Safe Travel

1. Tie down each canoe separately. Run two ropes or straps over the canoe's belly and secure each to its respective crossbar.

2. Add two lines to the bow and two lines to the stern of each craft. Secure each line to eyebolts in the bumpers, to padded S-hooks that ride in secure notches under the bumpers, or to loops of webbing secured to bolts under the hood (figure 4-5). Pull the webbing up through the crack between the hood and fender when you need it.

3. Don't use rubber ropes or bungee cords to secure canoes on cars!

4. Check the tightness of straps and ropes every time you stop for gas.

5. If you observe an unsafe cartopping situation, politely call it to the attention of the driver.

6. Caution: do not over-tighten the bow and stern lines on Kevlar and wooden canoes. Too much pressure can bend or break these boats. Experienced paddlers consider it safe to omit the stern (tail) lines on short, low profile canoes (most solo canoes). The exception is in high winds or when canoes are carried on cars that have closely spaced roof racks.

CHAPTER 5

How to Paddle Your Canoe

The Basic Strokes

Somewhere among the pages of every elementary canoeing text you'll find these time-worn admonitions: Be *careful* when approaching rapids and falls; and don't paddle dangerous waters until you've had some *experience*.

Caution and experience—sound advice for a safe, event-free canoe trip. Don't you believe it!

Some years ago, I helped rescue two canoeists who had inadvertently paddled over a 12-foot falls in Quetico Provincial Park, Ontario. They survived, but their canoe didn't! It was a classic example of a canoeing accident that could have ended in disaster. Both men used *caution* when they approached the

Jim Mandle, the author's friend, exhibits perfect form as he twists down a creek in the Adirondacks. The canoe is a Curtis Vagabond.

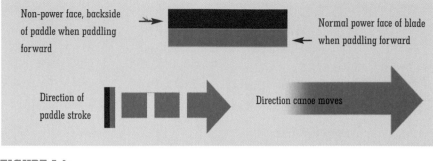

FIGURE 5-1:

Diagrams in this book will use this identification system.

falls, and by their admission, were *experienced*. They just didn't know how to paddle! For a decade they had repeated the same errors with no bad effects. Then came the falls.

As the case illustrates, simply paddling a lot won't teach you the correct way to canoe. What will is an understanding of the basic strokes and procedures.

Forward Stroke
(Used in both bow and stern)

Here's a stroke everyone thinks he or she knows (see figure 5-2). Just dip the blade in the water and pull back. Right? Almost. Fact is, the forward stroke is so sophisticated that canoe racers spend a good part of their lives attempting to perfect it. A few moments spent in a racing canoe with a pro will instantly dispel any illusions of simplicity you may have about this stroke.

Begin the forward stroke as close to the canoe as possible and as far forward as you can without lunging. Keep your top hand low—below your eyes—and push! Most of the power is in your top hand; your bottom hand functions mostly as a guide.

Pivot your shoulders with the stroke so the paddle comes straight back, *parallel* to the keel. Don't follow the curve of the gunnel! When your lower hand reaches your hip, take the paddle out of the water and begin a new stroke. Bringing the paddle too far back wastes energy and in fact slows the canoe. This is because a paddle blade brought

Start of forward stroke

Finish of forward stroke

FIGURE 5-2:

Forward Stroke: Put your paddle in the water about two feet in front of your body. Keep your top hand low—below your eyes.

beyond vertical pushes water up, which forces the canoe down into the water and slows its speed. This is why bent-shaft paddles—those with blades angled forward 12 to 14 degrees—are more efficient than straight ones. At the end of the stroke, the angled blade points down. No water is raised, no speed is lost.

Return the paddle to its starting position by "feathering" (turning the blade parallel to the water). This is especially important in wind.

The most common mistake beginners make is to paddle across their bodies. The paddle shaft *must* be perpendicular to the water, not at an angle to it.

Back Stroke
(Used in both bow and stern)

Most canoeists learn this stroke out of necessity when a rock looms ahead. It's one of the earliest strokes taught—and perfected—in white-water canoeing.

Rotate your shoulders and begin the stroke as far back as you can, using a levering action of your arms to pull the paddle through the water. Beginners will attempt to bring the paddle shaft across their bodies, which halves the energy of the stroke. The paddle shaft should be dead vertical.

Whitewater paddlers prefer an alternate form of this stroke, which is nothing more than a draw stroke (see following discussion) applied parallel to the keel line.

To perform this alternate stroke, twist your shoulders a full 90 degrees toward your paddle side and look toward the stern of the canoe. Draw water forward, toward the bow. This "back draw" is extremely powerful and blends instantly into the conventional draw, which is essential for correcting the ferry angle of a canoe in a strong current (see discussion in chapter 6).

Draw Stroke
(Used in both bow and stern)

Old canoeing publications recommended the bow rudder stroke for turning toward the paddle side. Now the bow rudder has been replaced by the much more powerful and versatile draw stroke (see figure 5-3).

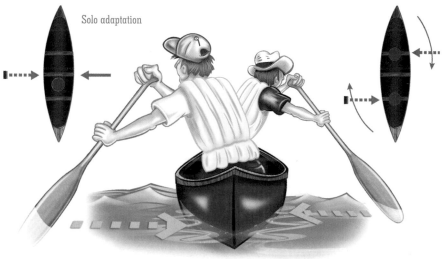

Solo adaptation

FIGURE 5-3:

Draw Stroke.

For maximum power and stability, execute the draw from a kneeling or well-braced sitting position. Reach as far out over the gunnel as you can and power the paddle inward, forcing water *under* the canoe. When the paddle comes to within 6 inches of the hull, slice it out (backward and up) and "draw" again. For maximum power, throw your body into the stroke.

The continuous power of the draw has a righting effect on the canoe and makes it almost impossible to capsize. However, once the power is released, you're at the mercy of gravity, so be sure your weight is well-centered in the canoe when the stroke is completed.

Cross Draw
(Used in bow only)

Basically an adaption of the old cross-bow rudder stroke, the cross draw (see figure 5-4) is nothing more than a draw stroke crossed over the bow of the canoe. Pivot at the waist, bring your paddle across the bow, reach far out . . . and draw. The canoe will turn smartly toward the paddle side.

The cross draw is a solo or bow stroke only. It cannot be done in the stern of a tandem canoe. It is extremely powerful; when coupled with a strong stern pry stroke (see below), the canoe will literally pivot

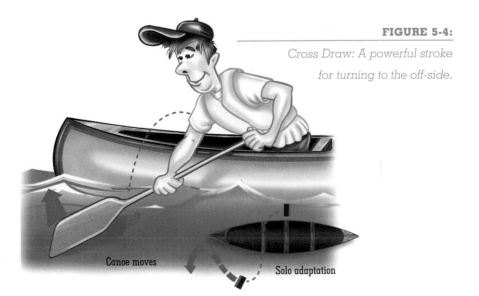

FIGURE 5-4:

Cross Draw: A powerful stroke for turning to the off-side.

Canoe moves

Solo adaptation

on its midpoint. The cross draw is also safe, as its shallow-running blade cannot catch on rocks and upset the canoe.

Pry (Pryaway)
(Used in both bow and stern)

The pry (see figure 5-5) is the exact opposite of the draw. Begin the stroke under the bilge of the canoe and lever the paddle blade smartly outward, using the gunnel or bilge for leverage. Use an underwater recovery for this stroke. The mechanics of this will be obvious once you've tried it.

Personally, I dislike the pry, as it's very hard on paddle shafts and gunnels. Like the draw, however, the pry has a strong bracing action during the power phase. For this reason, it is preferred over the cross draw for turning the canoe in heavy rapids.

Warning: Don't use this stroke in shallow water. The paddle blade might catch on a rock and capsize the canoe!

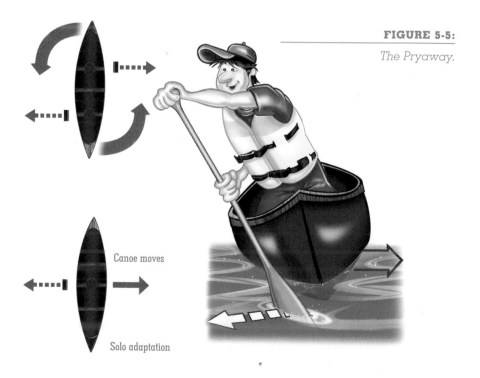

FIGURE 5-5:

The Pryaway.

Canoe moves

Solo adaptation

FIGURE 5-6:

The J-Stroke.

Start

Finish

Thumb of top hand is turned down.

J-Stroke
(Used in stern only)

Beginners quickly learn that canoes don't paddle straight unless they are ruddered. A canoe moving forward veers away from the stern person's paddle side. Put her in reverse and the opposite applies.

The J-stroke is the traditional way to correct the problem. Begin the J as a typical forward stroke and finish with a gentle "kick" outward (figure 5-6).

There are a number of variations on the J. Some paddlers begin with a conventional forward stroke, but shortly after the blade enters the water, they start turning the thumb of the top hand down (away from their body), which changes the pitch of the blade. The amount of pitch is increased so that by stroke's end the blade is in a rudder position, thumb of top hand pointing straight down. If additional correction is necessary, a slight outward pry (J) will do the trick. The more pry, the greater the correction. This *pitched-J* or *pitch stroke* is the most powerful and efficient of the various J-strokes.

Whitewater paddlers prefer a "thumbs-up" stern pry to the J because it quickly converts to a powerful pry, brace, or reverse sweep. Power forward, then quickly turn your grip hand "thumb straight up" at the end of the stroke. Rudder as needed to correct the course.

When going backwards, the bow person has the most paddle leverage and so should use a reverse-J to correct the course.

Minnesota Switch or Hut Stroke
(Used by both partners simultaneously)

The Minnesota switch or hut stroke (see figure 5-7) was first used in the 1940s by Eugene Jensen and Tom Estes to win a series of canoe races. Instead of using the conventional J-stroke to maintain a straight course, Gene and Tim simply switched paddle sides on cue. Every six to eight strokes, Tom would yell "Hut," and the two would trade sides. Over the years the stroke grew in popularity until today it is the preferred method

FIGURE 5-7:

The Minnesota Switch: Switching sides is easy as 1-2-3. If correctly done, only a split second is lost.

for traveling fast. Virtually every competitive canoe racer uses it (with bent-shaft paddles, of course!), to the complete exclusion of the J.

The Minnesota switch is very efficient—just what you need for trucking into the waves of a wind-tossed lake. But the canoe runs less than arrow-straight—the reason why traditionalists don't like it.

Sweeps
(Used in both bow and stern strokes)

Sweeps are useful in flat-water maneuvers for turning the canoe in a graceful arc. But compared to the powerful draw, cross draws, and prys, they are very inefficient. Nonetheless, they are part of the canoeing repertoire. See figures 5-8, 5-9, and 5-10.

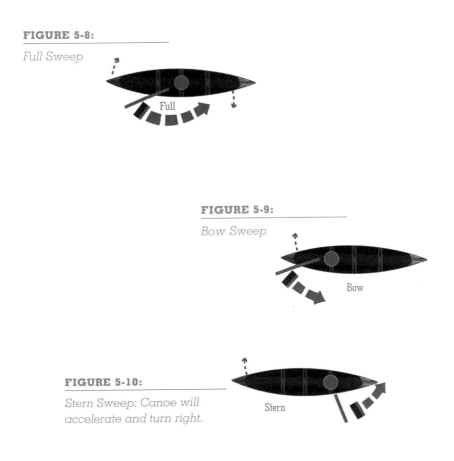

FIGURE 5-8:

Full Sweep

Full

FIGURE 5-9:

Bow Sweep

Bow

FIGURE 5-10:

Stern Sweep: Canoe will accelerate and turn right.

Stern

Stern Pry
(Used in stern only)

This is similar to the reverse stern sweep except that only the outward portion of the arc is completed.

For greatest leverage, begin the stern pry as far back as possible. Thrust the blade outward with a snappy levering action of your arms, perhaps prying the paddle shaft off the gunnel or your thigh (if you're seated). Combine this stroke with a powerful cross draw at the bow (figure 5-11a), and the canoe will pivot on its midpoint. Use a draw at the bow instead (figure 5-11b), and the canoe will slip sideways.

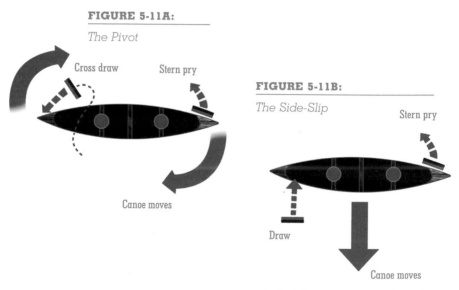

FIGURE 5-11A:

The Pivot

Cross draw   Stern pry

Canoe moves

FIGURE 5-11B:

The Side-Slip

Stern pry

Draw

Canoe moves

Similar to the reverse sweep except only the
outward portion of the arc is completed

Sculling Draw
(Used in both bow and stern)

The sculling draw (see figure 5-12) is used to move a canoe sideways in water too shallow to effect a good draw. It's also a nice stroke in "heavy water" (powerful waves), as it has a strong bracing effect. The sculling draw is hard to describe, easy to do, and fascinating to watch. Perform this stroke in front of onlookers and you'll instantly achieve expert status.

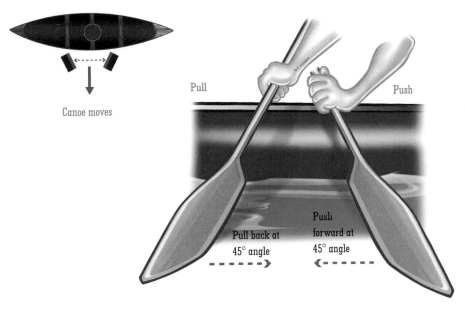

Pull

Push

Canoe moves

Pull back at
45° angle

Push
forward at
45° angle

FIGURE 5-12:

The Sculling Draw.

Place the paddle in the water a comfortable distance from the canoe, about 2 feet forward of your body. Rotate the leading edge of the paddle (normal power face of the blade) 45 degrees away from the canoe, and while maintaining this blade angle, pull the paddle backward. At the end of the stroke, rotate the leading edge of the blade a full 90 degrees, and using the same power face of the blade, push the water forward. The canoe will scoot toward your paddle.

The sculling draw is sometimes called the *figure-8 stroke* because the paddle describes this number as it is pulled through the water. That's inaccurate, however, as the path of the blade is nearly parallel to the keel line of the canoe.

A *reverse sculling draw* will cause the canoe to move away from your paddle side.

Jim Mandle, an American Canoe Association instructor, executes a perfect low brace in his restored 1910 Rushton "Indian Girl" canoe.

Low Brace
(Used in both bow and stern)

The low brace (see figure 5-13) functions as an outrigger to stabilize the canoe in turns and to keep it from capsizing in big waves. Reach far out, paddle laid nearly flat on the water, palm of top hand up. Put your weight solidly on the paddle—a half-hearted effort isn't good enough. If you're capsizing, a powerful downward push will right you. The push should be fast and smooth. If the canoe is moving forward, raise the leading edge of the blade so the blade is at a slight climbing angle to the oncoming water. Bear down on the paddle: The resultant "planing effect" will stabilize the canoe.

The low brace is essential for turning into or out of eddies (see chapter 6) and anytime you need to check a strong inside turn. Use it when you find yourself capsizing on your "on" (paddle) side.

High Brace
(Used in both bow and stern)

There are times when you need a strong brace, a draw, and a canoe lean all at once. Enter the high brace (see figure 5-14). It's nothing more than a stationary draw with the power face of the paddle held against the current or at a strong climbing angle to it. Success depends on speed—either paddling or current—and a strong lean to offset the pull of the moving water. The high brace blends easily to the draw—an essential stroke for pulling into eddies and making sharp turns. It can keep you from capsizing on your "off" (non-paddle) side.

FIGURE 5-13:

The Low Brace: Use this if you are capsizing on your "on" (paddle) side.

FIGURE 5-14:

The High Brace: Use this if you are capsizing on your "off" (non-paddle) side.

The Solo-C
(Used in solo canoe)

The Solo-C (see figure 5-15) is the lone paddler's J-stroke; it's the only way to keep a canoe on course without adopting the Minnesota switch.

Begin the stroke with a diagonally applied draw, then arc the paddle inward, *under* the canoe. Finish with a gentle outward thrust, not the powerful kick used in the J. Best results will be obtained if you progressively increase the pitch of the blade throughout the stroke. In the end, the thumb of the top hand should be turned straight down to facilitate this.

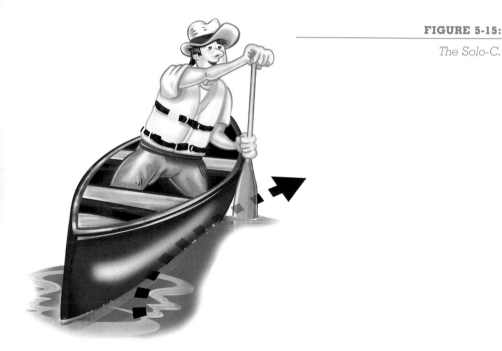

FIGURE 5-15:

The Solo-C.

CHAPTER 6

Canoeing in Whitewater and Currents

We put ashore just above the drop, then walked a well-worn trail to the high rock outcrop that overlooked the rapid. Two college kids stood near the precipice effusively describing their plans to power around the big rock (figure 6-1). I blotted out their mindless chatter and gathered my teenage crew around me.

"Don't listen to those guys," I admonished quietly. "It's a piece of cake if you can ferry and a sure wipeout if you can't. Here's the plan: Soon as you clear the tree, kick the tail to

Running rapids is safe and fun, if you know what you're doing. Note that these experienced paddlers are kneeling (for control and stability). The helmets are in case they capsize and are dashed against a rock. The canoe is a Dagger Legend.

the right and back-paddle furiously. If the stern person is paddling on the left, a hard stern pry will bring the tail around. If the stern's paddling on the right, a draw at each end will do it. As soon as you've set the angle, back-paddle—hard! You'll scoot sideways across the river into the clear channel at right. If you mess up and miss the ferry, you're done for!"

Any Questions?

While we were talking, the college boys shoved off into the current. Within seconds it was over. The inexperienced team broadsided the rock and capsized. Now two men and piles of camping gear were in the frothy water. But there was no real danger; the pair floated safely to quiet water below and were helped ashore by a half-dozen excited teenagers.

When the way was clear, my crew began its descent. We coasted beyond the downed tree, ferried right, then scooted into the clear channel exactly as planned. It was a classic textbook maneuver and we earned grade A all the way.

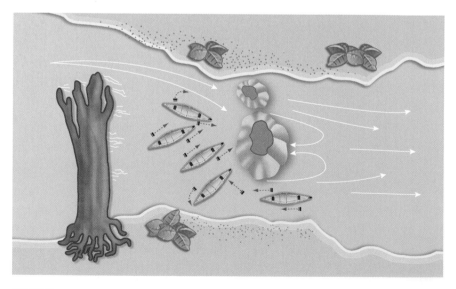

FIGURE 6-1:

Back-ferry to safety (small arrows indicate direction of paddle movement).

I smugly congratulated myself for the two days of training I'd given this crew before the trip. But best of all was seeing the look of envy on the faces of those dripping wet young men when two fourteen-year-old girls artfully negotiated the drop, then did a perfect stern-first landing within yards of their still swamped canoe. There was no denying that an ounce of skill outweighed a ton of macho!

Back-ferry, forward ferry, and in time, the eddy turn. These are the techniques you must master if you plan to negotiate complex currents. As the example illustrates, you cannot overpower a river. But with the right skills, you can outfox it. Here's how!

Learn to Ferry!

Ferrying across currents is nothing new. Even the ancient Egyptians were experienced in the art. They simply set the nose of their barge at 30 degrees to the current and powered ahead. The two vectors—forward speed of the boat plus sidewash of the current—carried them sideways across the river.

Whether you nose forward (the forward ferry—figure 6-2) into currents or back-ferry instead, depends upon the circumstances. In tight quarters, where quick turns are impossible, the back-ferry is preferred; for crossing large expanses of open water, the head-on approach is recommended. Ferrying is a game of skill, not brute power. Here are the rules for safe passage:

1. First, master the strokes outlined in the previous chapter. It's pointless to practice ferry maneuvers with your craft until you've learned to control the engines.

2. A ferry angle of around 30 degrees to the current is recommended. Less than this wastes energy, while more is difficult to maintain. There is a trigonometric relationship between the efficiency of the ferry angle and the downstream slip. In strong currents, it may be necessary to angle a full 90 degrees to the river's flow to get to the other bank with a minimum of downstream slide. However, 45 degrees is about the maximum angle of attack that most canoeists can hold. Since the penalty for "losing your angle" in a tough

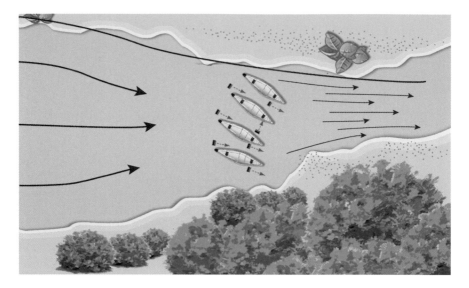

FIGURE 6-2:

Crossing a river using a forward ferry (arrows indicate direction of paddle movement).

current is broadsiding—and possibly capsizing—you'll want to maintain a cautious approach. I usually test strong currents with a 15- to 20-degree angle. As confidence builds, I widen the angle, adding or subtracting as the need arises. Figure 6-2 shows the relationship.

3. Watch the shore when you ferry across large expanses of water. It's very difficult to maintain the correct angle without referencing your progress to a land marker of some sort.

4. The canoe must be trimmed dead level or slightly lighter at the *upstream* end. It requires a very strong team to back-ferry a tail-heavy canoe!

5. When ferrying forward, the stern has more paddle leverage than the bow. When back-ferrying, the opposite is true. This means that the *downstream* paddler has the greatest responsibility for correcting the ferry angle.

Once you learn to perform competent ferries, you'll discover all sorts of applications for the technique. Here are a few:

Landing in Currents

Rivers run fastest at the center and slowest near the banks, so if you attempt to land nose-first, the current will grab your tail and spin downstream. In slow currents, the result is an uncontrolled eddy turn (figure 6-5 shows a "controlled" eddy turn)—the mark of a novice. On a fast river, it's a neck-snapping spin and a possible capsize!

For these reasons, it's almost always best to back-ferry to shore. Simply tuck your tail in the direction you want to go, then paddle backward. The harder you paddle, the more speed you'll scrub off. Ultimately, your stern will slide into the quiet water near shore, and your bow will follow suit. Easy as pie and guaranteed to elicit admiration from your friends.

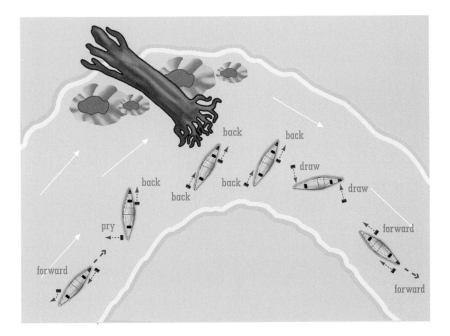

FIGURE 6-3:

Ferrying around a Sharp Bend: Keep away from the outside of the bends, except in low water (arrows indicate direction of the paddle movement).

Negotiating Bends

Rivers flow fastest on the outside bends, which is the reason why novice canoeists are often swept tail first into them. So if you want to maintain control of your canoe in a tight curve, you'll have to back-ferry around it. Figure 6-3 shows the procedure.

Parallel Side-Slip

In very slow currents where a ferry is overkill, a simple side-slip maneuver may often do the trick. Strokes? Bow person draws while his partner pries, or vice versa (see figure 6-4).

You'll quickly learn that you can't side-slip the average cruising canoe very far very fast, so rely on this maneuver for short distances only. A few inches of left or right side-slip is often enough to get you safely around a dead-ahead rock. Ferry and side-slip tactics are your best bet for avoiding the obstacles in a river.

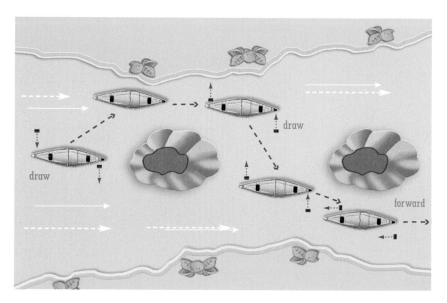

FIGURE 6-4:

The Side-Slip: You can't side-slip the average cruising canoe very quickly, so use this maneuver for short distances only.

Eddies Are a Safe Resting Place

Whenever water flows around a rock (but not over it!), a gentle upstream current, or eddy, is formed. Paddling through long stretches of rapids can be nerve-wracking: The quiet water of an eddy is a convenient place to rest and collect your thoughts.

Since the movement of water within an eddy is opposite to that of the river's flow, there is a current differential at the eddy's edge. This is the eddy line, and crossing it in strong currents can capsize you if you're not prepared for the consequences. If you cautiously poke your bow into the slow upstream current, the main flow of the river will catch your stern and spin it quickly downstream, as if a rug were pulled from beneath you. The result is a possible swim!

There are two ways to enter an eddy: by back-ferrying (the safest procedure), and by doing an *eddy turn* (the preferred method, once you learn the skills).

In figure 6-5, the bow person "hangs on" to the calm water of the eddy with a high brace and lean, while the stern person—who has not yet crossed the eddy line—also leans right to offset the centrifugal force. As soon as the turn is completed (it takes a split second), the pair paddles up to the rock.

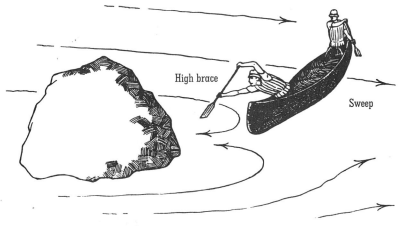

High brace

Sweep

FIGURE 6-5:

An Eddy Turn with a High Brace on the Inside: Canoe must be leaned upstream when the bow crosses the eddy line.

FIGURE 6-6:

An Eddy Turn with a Low Brace on the Inside: Bow person may use a pry, as illustrated (preferred), or a cross draw to turn the canoe into the eddy.

FIGURE 6-7:

The Peel-Out: Canoe enters the current at about a 45-degree angle. Bow paddler uses a high brace and leans the canoe downstream as the bow crosses the eddy line.

If, however, the partners were paddling on opposite sides, the roles—but not the canoe lean—would be reversed. Figure 6-6 shows the relationship.

Leaving an eddy (the *peel-out*) is simple enough if you remember to lean downstream. In figure 6-7 the canoe is angled at least 45 degrees to the current (a steeper angle than is used for back-ferrying) and power is applied.

As the bow crosses the eddy line, the bow person high-braces and leans downstream. The stern supports the lean and sweeps the canoe around. Figure 6-8 shows the procedure when paddle sides are reversed.

What about leaving an eddy by paddling out the weak lower end? In weak currents, that's possible; in big rapids the upstream current may be too powerful to overcome. Besides, small rocks often accumulate below large ones, which may prevent your leaving the eddy at the bottom end. Learn the eddy turn. It's an essential part of river canoeing!

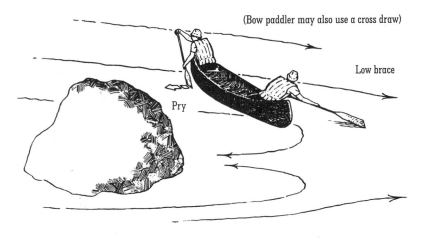

(Bow paddler may also use a cross draw)

Low brace

Pry

FIGURE 6-8:

The Peel-Out: Using a low brace on the downstream side, the bow paddler stabilizes the canoe with either a pry (illustrated) or a cross draw as the current spins it downstream.

Choosing a Safe Course Through Rapids

Negotiating a complex rapid without incident requires skill, cool determination, an accurate appraisal of the dangers, and a good partner. Here are the tenets of survival:

1. An upstream vee indicates the location of rocks; a downstream vee is the safe approach (figure 6-9).
2. You can't steer around obstacles in a fast-moving river: Rely instead on the ferry techniques and side-slip maneuvers explained in the last chapter.
3. Scout rapids from shore before you run them, and view everything from a downstream vantage point. Often, a substantial ledge that is invisible from above will be immediately apparent from below.

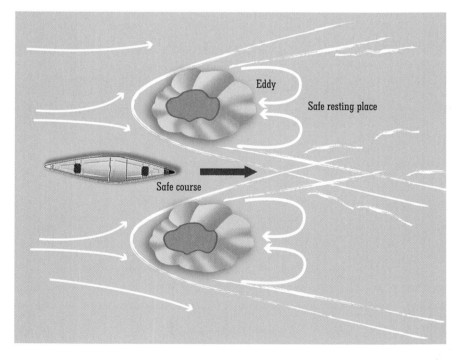

FIGURE 6-9:

Choose a safe downstream vee when entering a rapid.

4. Proceed downstream *slowly*—backpaddle to reduce speed. Maintain control with effective draws, prys, cross draws, and ferry techniques.

5. Take advantage of eddies to recover your strength and plan your strategy for the water ahead.

Negotiating a complex rapid without incident requires skill, cool determination and an accurate appraisal of the dangers. The paddler, Dennis Davidson, has turned right out of the current and is just nosing into an eddy. The canoe is a Royalex Dagger Ocoee.

Haystacks

When the fast water racing through a chute reaches the calmer water below, its energy dissipates in the form of nearly erect standing waves called haystacks. A series of uniform haystacks indicates deep water and safe canoeing—that is, if they're not so large as to swamp the canoe. To help the bow lift over large haystacks, slow the canoe's speed by backpaddling, or quarter into waves at a slight angle. You can also lighten the ends (you should lighten both ends, not just the bow!) by moving the paddlers closer amidships. If haystacks are very big, paddle the "edges" to keep from being swamped.

CHAPTER 7

Hazards

Hazards Canoeing in a Rough Sea

Running downwind: Running downwind on the crest of high waves is exhilarating but not always safe. The danger comes when the sea takes control and you begin to surf. Fortunately, canoes don't surf very well for very long. Invariably, the wave—and the scary ride it produces—will quickly pass. It's when a rocky shoreline looms ahead that you need to act fast. First, pour on the coal, which in itself is often enough to set you free. Failing this, bring the canoe to full speed then turn snappily into the wave (broadside it!). Brace hard on your paddles as the boat comes around and *lean downwind*. Don't be surprised if you take a few gallons of water aboard.

A very good team can sometimes backpaddle off the wave without "losing it." Try this with uncertain skills, however, and you'll capsize for sure!

Some authorities suggest you lighten the stern in a following sea to prevent waves from swamping the canoe at the tail. In truth, if you simply maintain forward speed (keep paddling!), you'll usually have no trouble. You absolutely must maintain momentum or you'll lose control!

If water splashes in astern you must lighten both ends of the canoe by moving paddlers together, closer amidships. Lightening just the stern isn't good enough: Canoes don't run

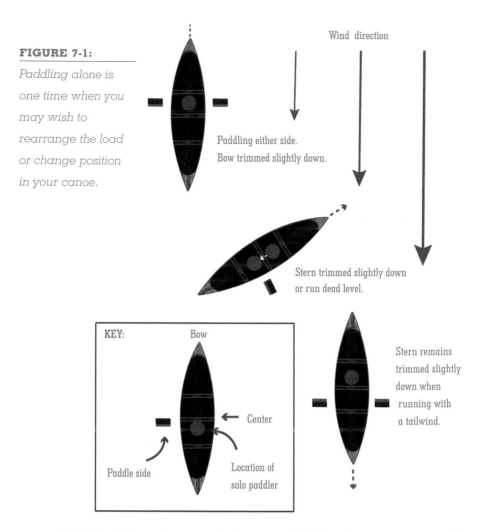

Wind direction

Paddling either side.
Bow trimmed slightly down.

Stern trimmed slightly down
or run dead level.

KEY:

Bow

Center

Paddle side

Location of
solo paddler

Stern remains
trimmed slightly
down when
running with
a tailwind.

well with their bows (or sterns) dragging. And they're not very controllable either.

Going upwind: Paddling upwind is much safer than going with the flow. To keep the bow from burying in big waves, lighten *both* ends. Paddle *straight into the waves*: Don't quarter them at an angle as recommended in most canoeing texts. Fact is, it requires an experienced team and a straight-keeled canoe to maintain a quartering angle in a rough sea. The penalty for broaching is a capsize! Use a fabric splash cover if you plan to canoe in heavy waves.

Loading for rough water travel: Canoes should be loaded dead level. Exceptions are racing and when paddling into or before a strong wind. Racing may require a *slightly* heavy bow to overcome the

The author paddles his pure-bred solo canoe (a Bell Wildfire) on Shoshone Lake, Yellowstone National Park, just after ice-out. Note the nylon spray cover which deters wind and waves, and the nearby ice chunks.

canoe's tendency to climb. Canoes will weathervane with the wind, so it helps if the windward end is trimmed lightly down (one inch is enough). You can push packs forward or back to adjust the trim or weight the windward end with a dry log. *Do not* use rocks—they could lodge under the deck or seat and cause the canoe to sink in a capsize! Remember: canoes don't handle well with one end dragging, so retrim (level) when you're back on calm water.

Paddling alone: This is another time when you may wish to rearrange the load or change positions in your canoe. Just remember that canoes will weathervane, and move forward or aft accordingly. Figure 7-1 shows the relationship. Be aware, however, that the farther you get from the center of the craft, the less control you'll enjoy. The best practice is to assume a central position in the canoe and rely on good paddling technique.

Never canoe alone from a position on the stern seat: It's akin to paddling a 7-foot canoe with a 10-foot overhang. The slightest puff of wind and over you'll go!

Soloists should always occupy a position within two feet of the geometric center of the canoe. In calm water, it's okay to sit on the front seat, facing backward. If you're really serious about soloing, you'll want a pure-bred solo canoe like the one in the photo.

Sweepers (Also Called Strainers)

A sweeper is a downed tree that wholly or partially blocks the flow of a river. It's one of the most dangerous of all river obstacles because its submerged branches can trap and hold a capsized swimmer or canoe. Even a very gentle current is strong enough to pin the most powerful swimmer in the branches.

Be particularly wary of sweepers that block outside curves, as the river's current will tend to force your canoe into them. If you capsize going into one of these brush piles and are trapped in the debris, escape—and rescue—may prove impossible!

The key to surviving an encounter with a sweeper is to avoid it! Hence, the importance of the *back-ferry*. If, despite your efforts, your canoe is carried into the branches of a fallen tree, keep calm, lean downstream, and don't grab anything until the canoe comes to complete stop. At this point, worrying over the canoe is futile. Save yourself (if you can) by climbing onto the tree trunk.

If you capsize and are sucked into the branches, try to go through head first so you can clear a path with your hands. Under these conditions, any loose-fitting clothing (including your life jacket) may get snared by branches and keep you from surfacing. So shed what you can, if you can!

Most of the spring drownings on rivers are the result of encounters with fallen trees. Learn to back-ferry around bends and you'll have no trouble with these obstacles.

Hypothermia

Hypothermia is a medical term that means "low body temperature." It's usually the result of capsizing in cold water or of paddling in an icy rain without proper clothing. Symptoms begin innocently enough, first with pronounced shivering (not a reliable indicator, since some people

Water temperature	Amount of time body will remain functional
less than 40 degrees F.	less than 10 minutes
40–59 degrees F.	15–20 minutes
50–60 degrees F.	15–40 minutes
60 degrees F. and above	one or more hours

lack the shivering reflex), followed by slurred speech and amnesia as the temperature drops.

At about 90 degrees Fahrenheit, shivering stops, muscles stiffen, and the skin becomes blue and puffy. Unconsciousness and erratic heartbeat follow. When the temperature drops below about 78 degrees Fahrenheit, death results.

The table shows the approximate amount of time the body can remain functional in cold water.

Numbers don't tell the whole story, however, as the shock of hitting the cold water in a canoe upset may cause a heart attack—the reason why you need to wear a neoprene wet suit or dry suit when you canoe frigid waters.

Treatment for hypothermia: Insulate the victim from the cold, wet environment. Replace wet clothing with dry, and administer *gentle, controlled* heat. The recommended procedure is to sandwich the stripped victim between two individuals of normal body temperature. Use a sleeping bag if you have one or pile on all the clothing you can find. You may administer warm drinks (no stimulants like coffee or alcohol) *only* if the victim can sit up and swallow.

Radiant heat from a fire is probably the quickest way to warm a victim of immersion hypothermia. However, radiant heat should be applied slowly and evenly. Excess temperature in a localized area may cause burns, as hypothermic persons have very little sense of feeling in their extremities. Treat a victim gently: roughhousing may cause heart fibrillation and death.

Hypothermia is emotionally and physically draining. Plan to camp for a full day after the experience to allow the victim to recuperate.

Dams and falls are something you look at, reverently photograph—and portage around! The falls are along the Kopka River, Ontario. The canoe is a Dagger Venture 17.

FIGURE 7-2:

It's unsafe to run any dam! The danger lies in the well-formed backroller that will trap your canoe and recirculate it with the eddy flow.

Dams and Falls

Low falls can be run if there's a strong enough flow and the drop is not so steep as to produce a *hydraulic jump* (heavy backroller) at their base. If, after checking the falls, you decide it's safe to run, pick the point of strongest water flow and proceed at river speed over the ledge. As you reach the base of the falls, dig your paddles hard and deep to climb out of the trough below.

It's unsafe to run *any* dam, unless, of course, part of it has broken away. The danger lies in the well-formed backroller at the base, which is essentially an eddy set on edge. These backrollers are "keepers": They'll trap your canoe and recirculate it with the eddy flow (see figure 7-2). Escape means diving deep below the eddy line to the main flow of the river, where you'll be jettisoned out—a technique that requires a cool head and in-depth knowledge of what is going on.

I know several people who have survived encounters with dams. All agree it was the most frightening experience of their lives. Their advice? "Don't run any dams. Ever!"

FIGURE 7-3:

Safest way to swim a rapid: Keep your feet high to prevent somersaulting in the current, and use your feet and paddle to ward off rocks. Do not try to stand in water that is over knee deep!

Self-Rescue

Everyone wants to be a hero and rescue someone. Fact is, in most canoeing accidents, you'll be rescuing yourself! Here are the suggested procedures:

Capsizing in rapids: Do not attempt to stand in water that is more than knee deep. A foot may become wedged between rocks and held there while the river mows you down. Entrapment is a major cause of drowning on fast-moving rivers.

Immediately upon capsizing, get to the upstream end of the canoe. Hold tight to the stern and *keep your feet high*, away from the river's bottom. Try to swim the boat to shore using a modified back-ferry technique. Stay with the canoe unless doing so will endanger your life.

If you're thrown clear of the canoe and are forced to swim, immediately get on your back, *feet held high* to prevent yourself from somersaulting in the current (figure 7-3). Your life jacket will keep you afloat. Use your feet and paddle to fend off rocks, which might otherwise take their toll on your body. Swim ashore by backstroking (back-ferrying).

The canoe grounds on a partially submerged rock: As the canoe runs up on the obstacle, the current will rapidly whip the stern end downstream. Act fast! *Lean downstream* and brace with your paddle until the canoe comes to a dead stop. If the craft spins 180 degrees, it will probably slide off the rock if the bow paddler shifts his/her weight downstream.

If the craft broadsides against the obstacle, follow this procedure: Keep the downstream lean! One partner should brace on the downstream side while the other attempts to work the canoe free. If the rock is large enough, the nonbracing partner should step out on it and free the canoe.

If the rock is submerged under the canoe's center, maintain the downstream lean as you shift your weight around to free the canoe. If the water is shallow (less than two feet deep), get out on the *upstream* side of the canoe and push off. Don't do this in deep water: the current will suck you right under the boat!

In summary:

1. Always maintain a downstream lean and brace when you ground on a midstream obstacle.

2. Get out on the upstream side of the canoe only if the water is shallow.
3. Get out on the downstream side of the canoe only if you can climb up on the rock.

Canoe-over-Canoe Rescue

If a canoe capsizes on reasonably calm water, you can perform a *canoe-over-canoe rescue*. Figure 7-4 shows the procedure. If you try the rescue in a current, be sure the rescue canoe is *upstream and perpendicular* to the swamped boat. As a final precaution, keep the "swimmers" upstream of the rescue boat, in the event the outfit plows into a rock. Here's the sequence:

FIGURE 7-4:

Canoe-over-Canoe Rescue.

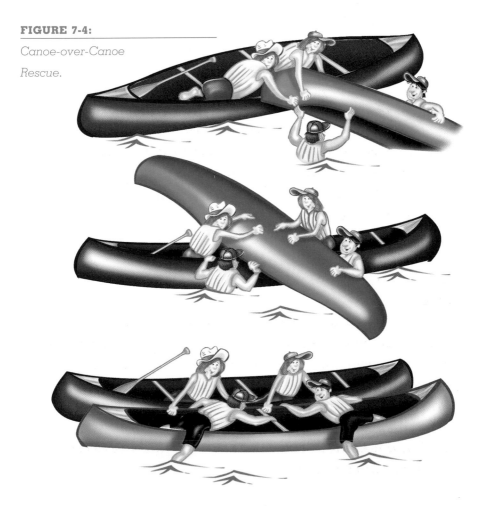

1. The swimmers work their way to the rescue canoe and stow their paddles inside it. Together, the four paddlers position the swamped canoe perpendicular to the rescue boat. The rescue team rolls the swamped canoe on edge to break the air seal. Then they lift the bow of the canoe up onto the near gunnel. If necessary, the swimmers push down on the stern end of the capsized canoe to help raise the bow.

2. The swamped canoe is drawn hand-over-hand across the gunnels, and the water is drained. Meanwhile, those in the water hold tight to the rescue boat.

3. The rescue team turns the canoe right-side-up and slides it back into the water. They then steady the craft while the upset paddlers climb aboard.

The entire process takes about three minutes.

Lightning

The often-quoted advice to get off the water when lightning strikes is sound. Unfortunately, this may not be possible if the shoreline is too unforgiving to permit a landing or if there is heavy, pounding surf.

Nonetheless, a lone canoe on open water is ripe for an electrical strike, so if you can't push ashore, take these precautions: There is a cone of protection that extends about 45 degrees from the top of the tallest trees or land masses. Stay within this cone of protection, but not so close that lightning could jump from the shore to you. Lightning can easily breach two dozen feet, so stay a few canoe lengths offshore as you work your way down the lake.

Since tree roots may act as an electrical conduit, be wary of large trees near the water's edge. Roots spread more horizontally than vertically, which increases the size of the danger zone.

There's a notion that canoes built of wood or fiberglass are safer than aluminum ones in an electrical storm. No way! In fact, the opposite may be true. Ships are occasionally struck by lightning, usually with no ill effect. That's because the electrical discharge passes from

Rescuing a capsized canoe with a canoe-over-canoe rescue. This technique is best reserved for calm water.

the ship's antenna or lightning rods around the hull and into the water. The metal skin of aluminum canoes may react similarly, provided that your mass is below the gunnels (so lay down in the boat!). Wood or fiberglass canoes may simply "fry."

All this is speculation, you understand. Best advice? Get to a shore... fast!

Canoeing Mistakes You Won't Want to Make!

Not scouting a familiar rapid: Round the bend you see the dancing horsetails of a familiar rapid. Pangs of conscience tell you to check the pitch from shore before you proceed, but you arrogantly dismiss the warning and plunge confidently ahead.

Then, you see it—a storm-downed sapling that blocks the way. The canoe spins sideways and overturns. Seconds later, the golden Kevlar hull is tightly wrapped around a midstream boulder. Safe on shore, you and your partner helplessly watch the craft break up.

Fantasy? Hardly! It happened to me on a Canadian river I'd paddled five times before. I thought I knew every rock and eddy in the water course. But it hadn't rained for weeks, and my ordinarily clear channel was a dry boulder bed!

Not scouting a rapid you've paddled many times is a canoeing mistake you won't want to make!

Wearing an unzipped life jacket: You're broiling from the heat of your life jacket, so you peel open the zipper to let in air. Ahh...cool at last.

Seconds later, you've capsized and are swept into the branches of a downed tree. The wings of your unsecured vest wag in the water and an armhole catches a tree branch. You stop with a jerk and are momentarily held under water. Thank God you're able to get free! Next time you go canoeing, you'll keep your life jacket zipped up tight!

Wearing high-topped shoes while canoeing a raging rapid: You have capsized in a shallow, powerful rapid and are thrown clear of the canoe. Instead of turning on your back, feet up (the "rapid swimming position"), you instinctively drop your legs and try to walk. Seconds later, a foot becomes lodged between rocks and the current mows you down. Luckily you're wearing low-quarter sneakers you can get out of!

Paddling barefoot: Sharp rocks, sticks, broken glass, and tin cans in the water can cause nasty wounds on bare feet. Protective footwear is a must if you have to step out of your canoe.

Forgetting to attach a security elastic strap to your eyeglasses: You *will* lose your eyeglasses in a capsize if you don't have a security strap!

Running rapids while wearing something around your neck on a cord: Some years ago, my friend's canoe upset on a bridge piling where the current speed was at least 15 miles per hour. He was wearing a Sierra cup on a string around his neck. The string caught on one of the canoe's yoke pads and held him under for nearly half a minute before it broke and set him free. For months afterward, his neck bore the scar of that capsize.

Never wear anything around your neck—camera, binoculars, or a strong necklace—that could stream out in a current and catch on obstacles! Also, be wary of pocket lanyards (on a Swiss Army knife, for example) that might catch on debris.

Sitting through a rapid when you should be kneeling: Well-anchored, widespread knees provide pressure points from which you can heel the hull right or left or brace far out with confidence. Don't be fooled by the success of down-river racers who never kneel in their canoes. The seats of racing canoes are slung too low for kneeling, and the bows are too narrow to spread your knees very wide.

Not treating life jackets as life-saving equipment: No one wants to wear a life jacket that is wet or torn. So *don't* sit on your life vest or leave it out in the rain when you're ashore. Rodents may munch on it, so don't leave it overnight under an overturned canoe. I keep my PFD inside my tent when I'm camping.

Not wearing polarized sunglasses: It's a canoeing axiom that the most difficult drops are always paddled into the sun. Polarized sunglasses that let you see rocks deep in the water are an essential part of whitewater canoeing!

Keeping the spare paddle in an accessible place: You're canoeing a rapid when your paddle breaks. You reach for the spare but it's tied to thwarts or buried under a mound of camping gear. Suddenly, a rock appears ahead. Bang! And, capsize!

Keep your spare paddle available! I'd rather leave it loose in the canoe, where it could float free and be lost in a capsize, than limit access by tying it to thwarts.

Setting a bent-shaft paddle on the ground, with the bend pointing down: Step on a "blade-down" bent-shaft paddle and you'll break it at the throat. Step on a "blade-up" paddle and the shaft will just lever skyward. Setting a bent-shaft paddle blade-down on the ground marks you as a novice!

Canoeing errors are endless. Each new paddle trip brings to light new ways to do things wrong.

Piling things too high in the canoe: A low load acts as ballast to stabilize a canoe in waves and rapids. A high one raises the center of gravity and makes the boat feel tippy. There's also danger that a "high item" might catch on a low overhanging branch or in a strainer if the boat capsizes. Packs should not protrude more than 10 inches above the gunnels.

Appendix 1:
Glossary of Canoeing Terms

amidships: The center or middle of a canoe.

bailer: A scoop (usually made from an empty bleach jug by cutting off the bottom) for dipping accumulated water from the bottom of the canoe.

beam: The widest part of the canoe.

bilge: The point of greatest curvature between the bottom and side of a canoe.

bow: The front end of the canoe.

broach: To turn suddenly into the wind.

broadside: A canoe that is perpendicular to the current of a river, thus exposing its broad side to obstacles in the water.

carry: See portage.

deck: Panels at the bow and stern of the canoe that attach to the gunnels.

depth: The distance from the top of the gunnels to the bottom of the canoe when measured at the beam (sometimes called center depth, as opposed to the depth at the extreme ends of the canoe).

draft: The amount of water a canoe draws.

flat water: Water without rapids, such as a lake or slow-moving river.

flotation: Buoyant material set into the ends (or other panels) of a canoe to make it float if upset.

foot brace: A wood or metal bar against which a paddler braces his or her feet. Foot braces help secure the paddler in the canoe and so add to the efficiency of his or her strokes.

freeboard: The distance from the waterline to the top of the gunnels at their lowest point.

gunnels (or gunwales): The upper rails of a canoe.

heel: When a canoe or boat leans to one side.

hogged: A canoe with a bent-in keel or keel line.

inwale: The inside portion of the gunnel.

keel: A strip of wood or aluminum that runs along the center bottom of the canoe.

leeward: A sheltered place out of the wind. Also, the direction toward which the wind is blowing.

line: Rope used to tie up a canoe or pull it around obstacles in the water. Also refers to working a canoe downstream around obstacles in the water with the aid of ropes (lines) attached to the bow and stern.

outwale: The outer portion of the gunnel.

painters: Lines attached to the bow and stern of a canoe.

planking: Lightweight boards nailed to the ribs on wood-canvas canoes. Its main purpose is to support the canvas.

portage: The physical act of carrying the canoe over land.

ribs: Lateral supports that run at angles to the keel on the inside of a canoe. Ribs provide hull rigidity and structural strength.

rocker: The upward curve of the keel line of a canoe.

skeg: A short vertical fin, like that used on the bottom of a surfboard.

skid plate: A piece of thick Kevlar that is glued to the bottom ends of a canoe. Prevents abrasion of the skin of the canoe.

splash cover: A fitted cover designed to keep water out of a canoe. Splash covers are useful in rough rapids and big waves.

stem: The extreme end of the canoe, below the decks.

thwart: A cross-brace that runs from gunnel to gunnel.

tracking: Working a canoe upstream, against the current, with the aid of ropes (lines) attached to the bow and stern.

trim: The difference in the draft at the bow from that at the stern of a canoe. A properly trimmed canoe will sit dead level in the water.

tumblehome: The inward curve of the sides of a canoe above the waterline.

waterline: The level to which water comes on the hull of the canoe when it is set in the water.

whitewater: Foamy (air-filled) turbulent water.

yoke: A special crossbar equipped with shoulder pads for portaging the canoe.

Parts of a Canoe

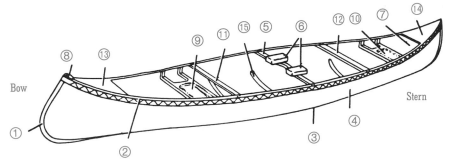

Key

1. Bang plate
2. Gunnel
3. Keel
4. Skin
5. Yoke
6. Yoke pads
7. Flotation

8. Towing link or shackle
9. Bow seat
10. Stern seat
11. Bow thwart
12. Stern thwart
13. Bow deck plate
14. Stern deck plate
15. Rib

Appendix 2:
River Rating Scale

Note: This nationally recognized scale, created by the American Whitewater Affiliation International, is used by whitewater canoeists to rate the difficulty of rapids. These ratings appear in many guidebooks and should be taken seriously. It's important to realize, however, that ratings change as water levels rise or fall. A rapid that rates Class I in midsummer may be a dangerous IV during the spring run-off. So plan your trips accordingly!

Water Class and Characteristics

I.   EASY—Easy bends, small rapids with low waves. Obstacles like fallen trees and bridge pilings. River speed less than hard backpaddling speed.

II.   MEDIUM—Fairly frequent but unobstructed rapids with regular waves and low ledges. River speed occasionally exceeding hard back-paddling speed.

III.   DIFFICULT—Small falls; large, regular waves covering boat. Expert maneuvering required. Course not always easily recognizable. Current speed usually less than fast forward-paddling speed. Fabric splash cover useful.

IV.   VERY DIFFICULT—High, powerful waves and difficult eddies. Abrupt bends and difficult broken water. Powerful and precise maneuvering mandatory. Splash cover essential!

V.   EXCEEDINGLY DIFFICULT—Very fast eddies, violent current, steep drops.

VI.   LIMIT OF NAVIGABILITY—Navigable only at select water conditions by teams of experts in covered canoes. Cannot be attempted without risk of life.

Index

haystacks, 68
hazards, 69–82
heel, defined, 84
high brace, 55, 63
high-top shoes, in
  rapids, 80
hogged, defined, 84
hull, displacement, 2
hut stroke, 50–51
hypothermia, 72–73
  treatment for, 73

inflatable canoes, 28
inwale, defined, 84

J-stroke, 49–50

keel, 3
  defined, 84
Kevlar canoe,
  19–20, 21
kneeling pad, 34

lay-ups, canoe
  chopper-gun, 22
  construction, 22
  hand, 22
leeward, defined, 84
length, of canoe, 2
life jacket, 31
  for children, 32
  as life-saving
    equipment, 81
  unzipped, 80
lift procedures, 37–42
  end lift, 39
  one person lift, 38
  two person lift, 39
lightning, 78–79
line, defined, 84
lining holes, 35

loading, for rough water
  travel, 70–71
longevity of, canoe,
  14–15
low brace, 54, 55

matt, defined, 21
Minnesota switch, 50–51
mistakes, in canoeing,
  79–82

neck, wearing some-
  thing around, on cord,
  80–81

one-person lift, 38
outwale, defined, 84

paddle, 29–30
  bent, 30
  bent-shaft, 81
  spare, 81
paddling, 43–56
  alone, 71–72
  back strokes, 45
  barefoot, 80
  basic strokes, 43–56
  bow sweep, 51
  cross draw, 47, 52
  draw stroke,
    46–47
  forward stroke,
    40–45
  full sweep, 51
  high brace, 55, 63
  hut stroke, 50–51
  J-stroke, 49–50
  low brace, 54, 55
  Minnesota switch,
    50–51
pivot, 51

pry (pryaway), 48
  sculling draw, 52
  side-slip, 52
  solo-C, 56
  stern pry, 52
  stern sweep, 52
  sweeps, 51
painters, defined, 84
parallel side-slip, 62
peel-out, from eddy,
  64–65
PFD (see life jacket)
pivot, 52
planking, defined, 84
polyester, in building
  canoe, 21
polyethylene canoe, 24
portage, 41
  cartopping, 41–42
  cinch sequence, 40
  defined, 84
  end lift, 39
  lift procedures, 37–42
  one-person lift, 38
  tie-downs, 39–41
  two-person lift, 39
pry (pryaway), 48

rapids, 57–68
  body position to
    negotiate, 81
  capsizing in, 76
  course through, 66–67
  familiar, not
    scouting, 79–80
  selection, 66
repair, ease of, 14
rescue
  canoe over canoe,
    77–78
  self, 76–77

About The Author

Cliff Jacobson is one of North America's most respected outdoors writers and wilderness guides. He is a professional canoe guide and outfitter, a wilderness canoeing and camping consultant, and the author of over a dozen top-selling books on camping and canoeing. His video, *The Forgotten Skills*, details the most important campcraft procedures. Cliff's methods are proven by the sweat of pack and paddle and are reminiscent of the days when skills were more important than things. A retired environmental science teacher (thirty-four years!), Cliff is respected by educators for his backcountry ethics, water quality, and wilderness navigation curricula. "The Wilderness Meal," an outdoor ethics unit he wrote for the Minnesota Department of Natural Resources, is among the most successful environmental education activities of all time. You'll find a copy in his book, *Boundary Waters Canoeing With Style*. In 2003 the American Canoe Association presented Cliff with the Legends of Paddling Award and inducted him into the ACA Hall of Fame.